# Intel Galileo
# Networking Cookbook

Over 45 recipes that will help you use the Intel Galileo
board to build exciting network-connected projects

**Marco Schwartz**

BIRMINGHAM - MUMBAI

# Intel Galileo Networking Cookbook

First published: August 2015

Production reference: 1240815

Published by Packt Publishing Ltd.
Livery Place
35 Livery Street
Birmingham B3 2PB, UK.

ISBN 978-1-78528-119-8

www.packtpub.com

# Credits

**Author**
Marco Schwartz

**Reviewers**
Tom Collins
Agus Kurniawan
Bharat Sesham
Alex Tereschenko

**Commissioning Editor**
Edward Bowkett

**Acquisition Editor**
Harsha Bharwani

**Content Development Editor**
Shweta Pant

**Technical Editor**
Narsimha Pai

**Copy Editors**
Dipti Mankame
Kevin McGowan

**Project Coordinator**
Sanjeet Rao

**Proofreader**
Safis Editing

**Indexer**
Hemangini Bari

**Graphics**
Sheetal Aute

**Production Coordinator**
Komal Ramchandani

**Cover Work**
Komal Ramchandani

# About the Author

**Marco Schwartz** is an electrical engineer, entrepreneur, and blogger. He has a master's degree in electrical engineering and computer science from SUPELEC in France and a master's degree in micro engineering from the EPFL in Switzerland. He has more than 5 years of experience working in the domain of electrical engineering. His interests gravitate around electronics, home automation, the Arduino and the Raspberry Pi platforms, open source hardware projects, and 3D printing. He runs several websites related to Arduino, including the Open Home Automation website, which is dedicated to building home automation systems using open source hardware.

He has written another book on home automation and Arduino, named *Arduino Home Automation Projects*, *Packt Publishing*. He has also published a book on how to build Internet of Things projects with Arduino, which is called *Internet of Things with the Arduino Yun*, *Packt Publishing*.

# About the Reviewers

**Tom Collins** is an entrepreneur, start-up enthusiast, and cofounder of AllThingsTalk. He received a first-class degree with honors and awards for his graduate exhibition on "The Convergence of Cloud Computing, Smart Devices and the Internet of Things". He has also developed SmartLiving.io project, assuming a jack-of-all-trades role spanning architecture, DevOps, full stack, and mobile development.

Tom's latest mission is to support innovation within start-ups and organizations through the IoT methodology, share toolkits, design patterns, and provide lessons to build IoT solutions.

**Agus Kurniawan** is an IT security and technology consultant, author, and lecturer. He has experience in various software development projects, producing material for training and workshops and producing technical writing for 14 years. He has been awarded the Microsoft Most Valuable Professional (MVP) award for 11 years in a row. He is involved in some research activities related to networking and security systems at the University of Indonesia. Currently, he's pursuing a PhD program in computer science in Germany. You can visit his blog at http://blog.aguskurniawan.net and his Twitter page at @agusk2010.

**Bharat Sesham** is enthusiastic and passionate about learning the latest technologies and applying them to solving real-life problems. He has participated in many reputed competitions; some of these are the Intel Embedded Challenge 2014, NASA Space Settlement Challenge 2013/2014, CANSAT 2015, Shell Idea 360 2015, which gave him a practical insight. He has a good knowledge of embedded systems, IoT, and OpenCV. Apart from this, he is also working for two start-ups based on OpenCV.

His blog site is https://bharatsesham.wordpress.com, and his Twitter page is @bharat_sesham.

I would like to thank Packt Publishing for providing this opportunity and I would also like to thank my parents for supporting and encouraging me throughout my journey.

**Alex Tereschenko** is an avid creator, who is sure that computers can do a lot of good for people when they are interfaced with real-world objects (as opposed to just crunching data in a dusty corner). That's what's driving him in his projects, and this is why embedded systems and the Internet of Things are topics he enjoys the most.

# www.PacktPub.com

## Support files, eBooks, discount offers, and more

For support files and downloads related to your book, please visit www.PacktPub.com.

Did you know that Packt offers eBook versions of every book published, with PDF and ePub files available? You can upgrade to the eBook version at www.PacktPub.com and as a print book customer, you are entitled to a discount on the eBook copy. Get in touch with us at service@packtpub.com for more details.

At www.PacktPub.com, you can also read a collection of free technical articles, sign up for a range of free newsletters and receive exclusive discounts and offers on Packt books and eBooks.

https://www2.packtpub.com/books/subscription/packtlib

Do you need instant solutions to your IT questions? PacktLib is Packt's online digital book library. Here, you can search, access, and read Packt's entire library of books.

## Why Subscribe?

- ▶ Fully searchable across every book published by Packt
- ▶ Copy and paste, print, and bookmark content
- ▶ On demand and accessible via a web browser

## Free Access for Packt account holders

If you have an account with Packt at www.PacktPub.com, you can use this to access PacktLib today and view 9 entirely free books. Simply use your login credentials for immediate access.

# Table of Contents

iii

# Preface

Intel Galileo is a great development kit for all your Do-It-Yourself electronics projects. The board has an in-built powerful Intel processor, but is usable with the well-known Arduino software. It is also compatible with most Arduino shields.

This makes it the ideal board for your projects, especially in the fields where you need to use cloud-based services, for example, to store data online. It is therefore a great board for Internet of Things (IoT) applications.

In this book, we are going to start setting up your board and building simple applications with the board, such as running a web server on the board. After this, we'll dive into more complex topics, such as IoT applications. Finally, we'll sum up everything we learned in the book by building a simple home automation system based on the Galileo board.

## What this book covers

*Chapter 1, Installing and Configuring Linux*, explains how to set up your Galileo board and the development environment, so you can start building projects. We will install the Galileo IoT image and install the required software on your computer.

*Chapter 2, Connecting External Sensors*, will discuss connecting sensors to the board, such as a temperature sensor. We will see how to read data from sensors and use it in our projects.

*Chapter 3, Controlling Hardware Devices*, covers how to control devices from the Galileo board, such as a relay that can be used to control electrical appliances.

*Chapter 4, Creating a Web Server*, is dedicated to running a simple web server on the Galileo board. We will see that a server can also be used to control the inputs and outputs of the board.

*Chapter 5, Hosting Applications on the Galileo Board*, covers how to host useful applications on the board, such as a simple file-sharing server.

*Chapter 6, Local Network Monitoring*, is dedicated to creating applications to monitor the activity of the Galileo board via the local network connection, for example, you will be able to monitor measurements done by the board in real time.

*Chapter 7, Cloud Data Monitoring*, is all about connecting your board to cloud services in order to build Internet of Things applications, such as remotely logging data on a cloud platform.

*Chapter 8, Building a Home Automation System*, sums up all that was done in the book with an application: building a home automation system based on Arduino, using the Galileo board as the "hub" of the system.

# What you need for this book

For this entire book, you will need an Intel Galileo board. In the first chapter of the book, you will learn how to install all the required software to configure your board.

You will also need a computer running Windows, Mac OS X, or Linux, as this will be needed to configure your Galileo board.

# Who this book is for

This book is intended for those who want to build exciting projects using the Intel Galileo board. It is for people who are already experienced in using more classic Arduino boards and want to extend their knowledge to the Intel Galileo board.

It is also for people who want to learn about electronics and programming, and Intel Galileo is the perfect platform for this.

# Sections

In this book, you will find several headings that appear frequently (Getting ready, How to do it, How it works, There's more, and See also).

To give clear instructions on how to complete a recipe, we use these sections as follows:

## Getting ready

This section tells you what to expect in the recipe, and describes how to set up any software or any preliminary settings required for the recipe.

## How to do it...

This section contains the steps required to follow the recipe.

## How it works...

This section usually consists of a detailed explanation of what happened in the previous section.

## There's more...

This section consists of additional information about the recipe in order to make the reader more knowledgeable about the recipe.

## See also

This section provides helpful links to other useful information for the recipe.

# Conventions

In this book, you will find a number of text styles that distinguish between different kinds of information. Here are some examples of these styles and an explanation of their meaning.

Code words in text, database table names, folder names, filenames, file extensions, pathnames, dummy URLs, user input, and Twitter handles are shown as follows: "Every time you see a line starting with `root@galileo`, this means we will be using the terminal."

A block of code is set as follows:

```
// Sensor pin
int sensorPin = 0;

void setup()
{

  // Start Serial connection
  Serial.begin(9600);
}
```

When we wish to draw your attention to a particular part of a code block, the relevant lines or items are set in bold:

```
// Sensor pin
int sensorPin = 0;

void setup()
{

  // Start Serial connection
  Serial.begin(9600);
}
```

Any command-line input or output is written as follows:

```
opkg install package_name
```

**New terms** and **important words** are shown in bold. Words that you see on the screen, for example, in menus or dialog boxes, appear in the text like this: "To solve this problem, simply push the **Reboot** button on the board."

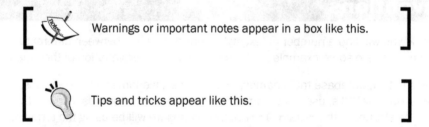

> Warnings or important notes appear in a box like this.

> Tips and tricks appear like this.

## Reader feedback

Feedback from our readers is always welcome. Let us know what you think about this book—what you liked or disliked. Reader feedback is important for us as it helps us develop titles that you will really get the most out of.

To send us general feedback, simply e-mail feedback@packtpub.com, and mention the book's title in the subject of your message.

If there is a topic that you have expertise in and you are interested in either writing or contributing to a book, see our author guide at www.packtpub.com/authors.

# Customer support

Now that you are the proud owner of a Packt book, we have a number of things to help you to get the most from your purchase.

## Downloading the example code

You can download the example code files from your account at `http://www.packtpub.com` for all the Packt Publishing books you have purchased. If you purchased this book elsewhere, you can visit `http://www.packtpub.com/support` and register to have the files e-mailed directly to you.

## Downloading the color images of this book

We also provide you with a PDF file that has color images of the screenshots/diagrams used in this book. The color images will help you better understand the changes in the output. You can download this file from `http://www.packtpub.com/sites/default/files/downloads/1198OS_ColorImages.pdf`.

## Errata

Although we have taken every care to ensure the accuracy of our content, mistakes do happen. If you find a mistake in one of our books—maybe a mistake in the text or the code—we would be grateful if you could report this to us. By doing so, you can save other readers from frustration and help us improve subsequent versions of this book. If you find any errata, please report them by visiting `http://www.packtpub.com/submit-errata`, selecting your book, clicking on the **Errata Submission Form** link, and entering the details of your errata. Once your errata are verified, your submission will be accepted and the errata will be uploaded to our website or added to any list of existing errata under the Errata section of that title.

To view the previously submitted errata, go to `https://www.packtpub.com/books/content/support` and enter the name of the book in the search field. The required information will appear under the **Errata** section.

## Piracy

Piracy of copyrighted material on the Internet is an ongoing problem across all media. At Packt, we take the protection of our copyright and licenses very seriously. If you come across any illegal copies of our works in any form on the Internet, please provide us with the location address or website name immediately so that we can pursue a remedy.

Please contact us at `copyright@packtpub.com` with a link to the suspected pirated material.

We appreciate your help in protecting our authors and our ability to bring you valuable content.

## Questions

If you have a problem with any aspect of this book, you can contact us at `questions@packtpub.com`, and we will do our best to address the problem.

# 1

# Installing and Configuring Linux

In this chapter, we will cover the following recipes:

- ► Configuring your Galileo for the first time
- ► Using a simple Linux image
- ► Using the IoT Linux image
- ► Accessing the Galileo board remotely
- ► Installing and updating modules
- ► Accessing Galileo via Wi-Fi
- ► Troubleshooting Linux installation issues

# Introduction

This first chapter of the book is focused on getting you started with Linux on your Intel Galileo board. You will learn how to set up your board out of the box. You will also learn how to install the different Linux images that you can install on the Galileo board. We will also learn how to install Linux on an external SD card that can be inserted into the Galileo board.

We are also going to see how to access a Galileo board remotely, and how to install new modules on it. Finally, we will see how to get rid of the Ethernet cable and use Wi-Fi to access the Galileo board.

 Note that all of the projects in this chapter and this book use the second generation Intel Galileo board. Several projects might work with a first generation type, but this is not guaranteed.

# Configuring your Galileo for the first time

The first step when you receive your Galileo board is to set it up. This is relatively easy but is a bit more complex than it is with other boards such as the Arduino. Therefore, we need to make sure that it is perfectly configured and set up before we move on to the other recipes in this chapter.

Inside the box, you will find the board itself and a power adapter that you can use to power up the board. You will also find a short manual about the board and the Intel Galileo platform.

## Getting ready

The first thing you will need is, of course, a Galileo board, which is shown here:

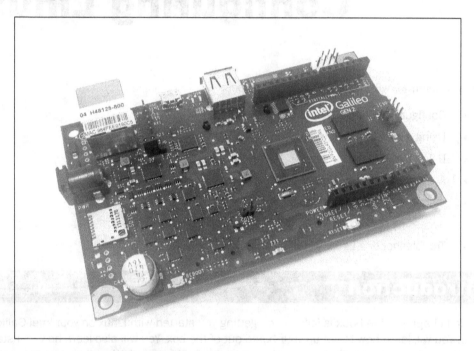

Note that you will need a Galileo Gen 2 board for the rest of this book. You might be able to follow along just fine with a Gen 1, but there might be some differences.

You can find a Galileo board on SparkFun:

```
https://www.sparkfun.com/products/13096
```

You also need an external power supply for your board, which is shown here:

This power supply is usually provided with the Galileo board but, if this is not the case, or you got your Galileo board separately, you will need to use the 12V DC power supply found in the box, or any other DC power supply in the 7V to 15V range.

Finally, you will also need a micro SD card, as shown here, which we will use in some projects in this chapter:

This SD card will be used to install the different Linux images, and also to store measurement data. I recommend an SD card with more than 2 GB of storage.

## How to do it...

Let's now assemble our Galileo board. These are the steps to follow to set up your Galileo board:

1.  Insert the micro SD card into the corresponding slot on the Galileo board.

2.  Insert an Ethernet cable from your router into the Galileo board.

3.  Connect the Galileo board to your power supply by connecting the DC jack.

This should be the result:

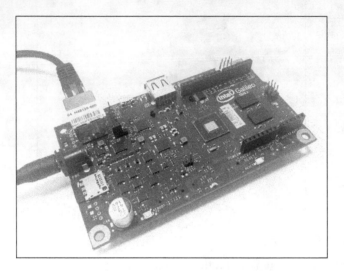

You will see that some LEDs light up when this is done.

## How it works...

The Galileo board basically needs three things to work correctly:

- ▶ The correct power supply
- ▶ A connection to your local network via Ethernet or Wi-Fi
- ▶ A micro SD card inserted into the board (this is not required for the basic operation of the board, but to install Linux images)

Having done this, we are then able to use our board for all the projects in this book.

## See also

This is really the foundation of the whole book, so make sure that you complete this recipe correctly. To go further, follow one of the two upcoming recipes to install Linux on your Galileo board.

# Using a simple Linux image

To really make use of the board and create exciting projects, we need to install a Linux image on our Galileo board. We will see that we have two options. The first one is the one we are going to see in this recipe—it is a simple Linux image, which is also simple to install. We will see how to install it in this guide.

## Getting ready

First, you have to make sure that you have followed the recipe at the beginning of this chapter, so you should have your board ready to be use.

Then you can get the Linux image from the following location:

`https://communities.intel.com/docs/DOC-22226`

You will be redirected to a page that contains a table with all the available downloads for the Galileo board:

Simply click on the first link and wait until the image is downloaded onto your computer.

## How to do it...

You are now ready to install the Linux image on your Galileo board. To do so, simply follow these steps:

1.  Unzip the contents of the file you just downloaded.
2.  Remove the micro SD card from the Galileo board.
3.  Insert the micro SD card into your computer.
4.  Format the SD card, if necessary, in the FAT32 format (if there are files on it already).
5.  Copy the contents of the Linux image to the SD card.
6.  Power down your Galileo board. You can also connect your board to your local network with the Ethernet cable at this point.
7.  Insert the SD card into your Galileo board again.
8.  Power the Galileo board up again.

The simple Linux image is now installed and running on your Galileo board.

## How it works...

The Galileo board will now boot every time on this Linux image, allowing you to access all the functions and modules that we listed earlier.

## There's more...

The Linux image that you just installed comes with many extras. This is a non-exhaustive list of all the features and modules that come with the Linux image:

- ▶ Wi-Fi drivers
- ▶ A Python interpreter
- ▶ SSH (to access your board via Ethernet)
- ▶ OpenCV (for image and video processing)
- ▶ Video4Linux2 (to record videos)
- ▶ **Advanced Linux Sound Architecture** (**ALSA**) drivers (to play sounds)
- ▶ Node.js (to run servers and applications based on JavaScript)

## See also

If you need an even more advanced image installed on your Galileo board, look at the following recipes to see how to install the **Internet of Things (IoT)** image.

# Using the IoT Linux image

Using the simple Linux image that we described in the previous recipe is great, but it can be quite difficult to use. You need to manually login to your board, and then use command lines to install new modules and run your applications. For example, you would have to use terminal software (such as PuTTY) to access the board.

Luckily for us, Intel has come up with a whole suite of software to allow you to code your application directly with a graphical interface, without typing a single line of code into a terminal. In this recipe, we are going to see how to install this software suite.

## Getting ready

This software suite comes in two parts— a new image, called the IoT image, that you need to install on the SD card, and also some software called (**Cross-Platform Development Kit**) **XDK** that needs to be installed on your computer.

The first step is to download this IoT image from the Intel website:

```
https://software.intel.com/en-us/iot/downloads
```

This is the page you will see when going to this web address:

Download the image from the web page. Then, go to the following address to download the Intel XDK software:

```
https://software.intel.com/en-us/html5/xdk-iot
```

You will be redirected to the page where you can download the Intel XDK software for your operating system:

## How to do it...

Installing the Intel IoT image is a bit more complex than it is with the simple Linux image. It varies depending on your operating system. Luckily for us, Intel has written guides to help install this image, depending on your operating system:

```
https://software.intel.com/en-us/iot/downloads
```

Simply follow the corresponding guide before continuing this recipe.

Installing the Intel XDK software is actually much easier. You simply need to execute the installer and just let yourself be guided by the instructions. When you first launch the software, you will be asked to create an account on the Intel website.

This is what the software looks like:

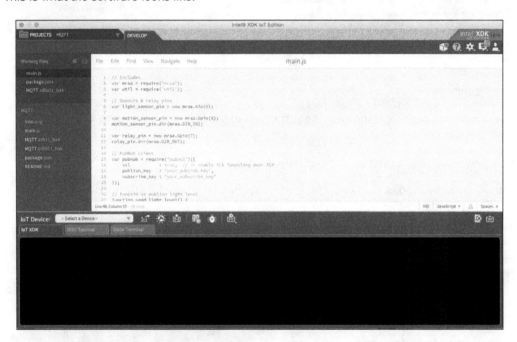

Congratulations, you are now completely ready to use the Intel IoT development suite on your computer!

## How it works...

The Intel IoT image and Intel XDK work together to make development on your Galileo board much simpler. XDK is able to locate your Galileo board automatically on your network, develop applications in Node.js inside the software, and then automatically upload and run these applications on your Galileo board!

## There's more...

You will see that the Intel XDK software offers much more than what we are going to use in this book. You can actually develop mobile applications that work on your phone and communicate directly with your Galileo board, right from Intel XDK!

You have other options to program your board at this point. The first option is to use Eclipse, which also lets you program the board, but by using C/C++ instead of Node.js. The next option is to use the special version of the Arduino IDE for the Galileo board, which lets you program the board with the well-known Arduino language.

## See also

Using this recipe will allow you to make nearly all the recipes in the subsequent chapters of this book. Look at the remaining recipes in this chapter to see how to access your board once the IoT image is installed.

# Accessing the Galileo board remotely

If you have followed one of the two previous recipes in this chapter, you now have a fully operational Linux image running on your Intel Galileo. Now, we are going to see what you can do with it. The first step is to verify that the installation was actually successful and that you can access your board remotely. To do that, we are going to use **Secure Shell** (**SSH**) to log in to your Galileo board remotely.

## Getting ready

You will need to have a Linux image installed on your Galileo board. I recommend using the IoT image for this, as this is the image we will be using in the rest of the book.

For the rest of this recipe, we will assume that the IoT image is installed and running on your Galileo board.

## How to do it...

The first step is to get the IP address of your board. This is important, as we will always use this IP to access your board. For your board to get a relevant IP address, it needs to be connected to the same local network as your computer.

To do so, the simplest way is to open the Intel XDK software. Log in, and then you will see, at the bottom part of the window, that you have a **Select a Device** menu. You should see your Galileo board in this menu, along with the IP address next to it, as shown in this screenshot:

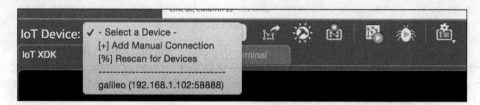

For this to work correctly, you also need to have Bonjour installed on your computer.

Now, go to a terminal to login to your board via SSH. If you are using Linux or OS X, you already have a terminal that you can use.

If you are using Windows, I recommend using PuTTY:

`http://www.putty.org/`

PuTTY is a basic type of terminal software for Windows that allows you to use the board remotely.

Now, go to a terminal and type in the following command by putting in the IP address of your board:

`ssh root@192.168.1.102`

You should see that you are logged in to your Galileo board:

```
macbookpro:~ marco$ ssh root@192.168.1.102
The authenticity of host '192.168.1.102 (192.168.1.102)' can't be established.
RSA key fingerprint is 7a:8b:27:d4:70:55:5d:2a:f8:e7:a8:7b:0a:14:be:4c.
Are you sure you want to continue connecting (yes/no)? yes
Warning: Permanently added '192.168.1.102' (RSA) to the list of known hosts.
root@galileo:~# 
```

If you can see these messages, it means you can successfully access your board via SSH!

## How it works...

SSH is a protocol to securely login to a remote Linux machine, such as the Galileo board, running a small Linux distribution. It allows you to control your board from any machine in your network, and install updates and new modules.

## There's more...

This is just the first step in using your Galileo board remotely. In the next recipes, we will use it for much more than just logging in, for example to install new modules and to run applications.

## See also

You should now go to the next recipe to learn how to install modules and install updates on your Galileo board.

# Installing and updating modules

So far, we have learnt how to access the board remotely via SSH, from any machine on your local network. Now, we are going to see what we can actually do with that. As we are still in an introductory chapter, we will see how to perform a simple operation—update the Linux modules that are already installed on the board, and install new ones.

## Getting ready

To follow this recipe, you need to have a Galileo board with a fully operational Linux image, on which you can access via SSH just as we did in the previous recipe. The Linux image you are using doesn't actually matter that much.

## How to do it...

Once you are logged in to your Galileo board via SSH, you are able to type commands directly into the terminal. Every time you see a line starting with `root@galileo`, this means we will be using the terminal.

If you are using the IoT image, the first thing you can do is type the command:

```
opkg update
```

This will update the list of available packages and updates for your Galileo board. This is the result inside the console:

```
root@galileo:~# opkg update
Downloading http://iotdk.intel.com/repos/1.1/iotdk/all/Packages.
Updated list of available packages in /var/lib/opkg/iotdk-all.
Downloading http://iotdk.intel.com/repos/1.1/iotdk/i586/Packages.
Updated list of available packages in /var/lib/opkg/iotdk-i586.
Downloading http://iotdk.intel.com/repos/1.1/iotdk/quark/Packages.
Updated list of available packages in /var/lib/opkg/iotdk-quark.
Downloading http://iotdk.intel.com/repos/1.1/iotdk/x86/Packages.
Updated list of available packages in /var/lib/opkg/iotdk-x86.
Downloading http://iotdk.intel.com/repos/1.1/intelgalactic/Packages.
Updated list of available packages in /var/lib/opkg/mraa-upm.
root@galileo:~#
```

Note that this also requires the Galileo board to be connected to the Internet, for example, by plugging it into your Internet router.

Now, you can actually update the packages themselves by typing:

`opkg upgrade`

This will automatically update all packages that need to be updated. Make sure you run it regularly, as Intel comes up with new versions of these packages all the time.

You can also use the package manager to install new modules. To see which packages are available, type:

`opkg list`

This will list all the available packages, as shown in this screenshot:

```
 Interface code.  This package contains documentation.
xz - 5.1.3alpha-r0 - Utilities for managing LZMA compressed files  Utilities for managing LZMA
 compressed files.
xz-dbg - 5.1.3alpha-r0 - Utilities for managing LZMA compressed files - Debugging files  Utilities
 for managing LZMA compressed files.  This package contains ELF    symbols
 and related sources for debugging purposes.
xz-dev - 5.1.3alpha-r0 - Utilities for managing LZMA compressed files - Development files
 Utilities for managing LZMA compressed files.  This package contains
 symbolic links, header files, and related items necessary for software
 development.
xz-doc - 5.1.3alpha-r0 - Utilities for managing LZMA compressed files - Documentation files
 Utilities for managing LZMA compressed files.  This package contains
 documentation.
xz-locale-cs - 5.1.3alpha-r0 - Utilities for managing LZMA compressed files - cs translations  Utilities
 for managing LZMA compressed files.  This package contains    language
 translation files for the cs locale.
xz-locale-de - 5.1.3alpha-r0 - Utilities for managing LZMA compressed files - de translations  Utilities
 for managing LZMA compressed files.  This package contains    language
 translation files for the de locale.
xz-locale-fr - 5.1.3alpha-r0 - Utilities for managing LZMA compressed files - fr translations  Utilities
 for managing LZMA compressed files.  This package contains    language
 translation files for the fr locale.
xz-locale-it - 5.1.3alpha-r0 - Utilities for managing LZMA compressed files - it translations  Utilities
 for managing LZMA compressed files.  This package contains    language
 translation files for the it locale.
xz-locale-pl - 5.1.3alpha-r0 - Utilities for managing LZMA compressed files - pl translations  Utilities
 for managing LZMA compressed files.  This package contains    language
 translation files for the pl locale.
root@galileo:~#
```

To install a given package, just type the following command, replacing `package_name` with the name of the package you want to install:

```
opkg install package_name
```

## How it works...

The `opkg` command installs the package manager (`opkg`) for the Intel Galileo Linux machine. It allows you to update your existing packages automatically and also install new packages on your Galileo board. In this way, you can always stay up-to-date and extend the functionalities of your board with new modules.

## There's more...

We only covered the basics of what the `opkg` tool can do. To see all the possibilities offered by the tool, type this into the terminal:

```
opkg -h
```

This will list all the commands and options offered by this tool.

## See also

Installing new packages and updating existing packages requires you to access your board remotely. So far we have done this via Ethernet, but you can check the next recipe to learn how to do it via Wi-Fi.

# Accessing Galileo via Wi-Fi

Using the onboard Ethernet port is great for accessing your Galileo board remotely. However, this is not always convenient. Most of our devices nowadays are connected wirelessly, and it can be strange sometimes to still use Ethernet cables.

This is why we are going to find out how to easily install a Wi-Fi board on the Galileo and then access the board remotely. You will then be able to complete all the projects in this book without ever connecting an Ethernet cable again.

## Getting ready

For this recipe to work, you will need to have followed most of the previous recipes in this chapter. You need a working Galileo board, with either the simple Linux image or the IoT image installed. You should also have checked that you can access the board via Ethernet first, to make sure that everything is working.

Then, you need a Wi-Fi board. I recommend using the Intel N-135 Wi-Fi board, which is very easy to install and will work out of the box. This is a picture of this board:

You can easily find it online, for example on Amazon, here:

`http://goo.gl/70UXFw`

It might be possible to use other Wi-Fi boards, but they could be more difficult to use or require the use of drivers to work. You can also use a Wi-Fi dongle that is compatible with the Galileo board.

## How to do it...

You can simply install the board by following all the steps in this section:

1. First, power down the Galileo board and remove all the connection cables.
2. Then, turn the board over and locate the mini PCI express port, as shown here:

3.  Insert the Wi-Fi card into the port at a small angle.

4.  After that, press it down until you hear a click, meaning the board was successfully installed.

5.  Connect all the cables to the Galileo board again and power it up.

Now that the Wi-Fi module is correctly installed, you will have some simple steps to follow to set up your Wi-Fi connection. Let's assume here that you have a WPA-secured Wi-Fi network, which is the case for most Wi-Fi networks, then follow these steps:

1.  Log on to your Galileo as `root`, just as you learned in the previous recipes in this chapter.

2.  Create the file that will contain your network's configuration by typing the following command, replacing `MySSID` with your Wi-Fi network name:

    ```
    # wpa_passphrase MySSID << EOF > /etc/wpa_supplicant.conf
    ```

3.  Then, type the following command, replacing `MyPassPhrase` with your Wi-Fi network password:

    ```
    > MyPassPhrase
    ```

4.  Finally, type:

    ```
    > EOF
    ```

This will connect your board to your Wi-Fi network. You can then follow these steps to connect it to your network automatically:

1.  Edit the `/etc/network/interfaces` file with `vi`.

2.  Add the line `auto wlan0`.

3.  Save, using the `:w` command followed by the `:q` command.

4.  Restart the wireless interface by typing:

    ```
    /etc/init.d/networking restart
    ifdown wlan0
    ifup wlan0
    ```

From now on, your Galileo board will automatically connect to your network using Wi-Fi. You need to take these steps again if you modify your Wi-Fi network name and/or password.

You can now remove the Ethernet cable and login to your Galileo board again via Wi-Fi.

## How it works...

The Galileo board mini PCI express port was made specifically to support extensions such as this Wi-Fi board. This port can be used to extend the possibilities offered by the Intel Galileo board.

## There's more...

You can use the mini PCI express slot that we used in this recipe for many extensions other than Wi-Fi. For example, there are specific extensions for Bluetooth 4.0, and for more SD card slots for additional storage.

# Troubleshooting Linux installation issues

In this last section of the chapter, we are going to see what can go wrong when configuring your board and installing Linux on it. Indeed, some of the steps involved here are quite complex and many things can work out differently than expected.

## How to do it...

Some of the most commonly faced issues working with the Intel Galileo board are as follows:

  ▶ **The board doesn't boot**: The first thing that can happen is that the board doesn't actually boot. If no LEDs light up at all, you have some serious problems. First, make sure that the power adapter you are using is working. Then, if the problem persists, it probably means your Galileo board has a problem, and needs to be replaced.

  ▶ **Installing the Linux image failed**: If you can't install the simple Linux image on an SD card, format the SD card first using your computer. It can be the case that there are files on the SD card or it was formatted using the wrong file format.

  ▶ **Installing the IoT image failed**: If, for any reason, the installation of the IoT image fails, the first thing to do is repeat the procedure. Also, make sure to follow step-by-step the instructions from the Intel website, as only missing a single step can lead to a problem with the SD card.

    You can also try to reformat the SD card before following the steps from the Intel website.

  ▶ **The board cannot be accessed remotely**: If you cannot log on to your board via SSH, first make sure that you are trying to access the correct IP address. Use the Intel XDK software for that. You can also try to ping the board from a terminal to make sure that it is answering network requests. Also, make sure that Bonjour is installed on your computer.

  ▶ **The package manager doesn't work**: The main reason for the package manager not working is that you are not connected to the Internet. Make sure that your Internet router is configured to share Internet access across all devices connected to it.

    Also, I noticed that the Galileo board sometimes just loses Internet connectivity. To solve this problem, simply push the **Reboot** button on the board.

▸ **New packages can't be installed**: If you are sure that your Internet connectivity is working, it could simply be that you are trying to install a module that is not available for the Galileo. Not all Linux packages are available, so make sure first that the desired package is available for the Intel Galileo board.

▸ **The board cannot be accessed via Wi-Fi**: If the Wi-Fi connection doesn't work, first make sure that the Wi-Fi extension board is correctly connected to the board. If the board doesn't show up on the Galileo board interface (as `wlan0`), there might be a hardware problem with the extension board.

# 2

# Connecting External Sensors

In this chapter, we will go through the following recipes:

- ▶ Using the Arduino IDE with the Galileo board
- ▶ Connecting an analog sensor
- ▶ Connecting a digital sensor
- ▶ Connecting an LCD screen
- ▶ Displaying the temperature on an LCD screen
- ▶ Troubleshooting the usual issues with sensors

## Introduction

In this chapter, we are going to learn how to connect sensors to your Galileo board. This is a very important chapter in this book, as we will be using sensors throughout the rest of the book, for example to log measurements to the cloud.

In this chapter, we are going to see how to connect commonly used sensors between Arduino systems and the Galileo board. We are going to see how to connect analog and digital sensors, as well as an LCD screen to display measured data.

# Using the Arduino IDE with the Galileo board

Before we take measurements from the sensors, we need to be able to develop software to run on our Galileo board. There are two ways to do that; either by using the Arduino IDE (which has been modified for Galileo) or by using the onboard Linux machine that we configured in *Chapter 1, Installing and Configuring Linux*. In this chapter, as we will deal with basic sensors, we are only going to use the Arduino IDE, and we will see how to use it in this first recipe.

## Getting ready

For this first recipe, you will need to get the Arduino IDE for Intel Galileo from the official page at `https://communities.intel.com/docs/DOC-22226`.

There, you have the choice between different versions of the Arduino IDE for the Galileo board, depending on your operating system:

**Arduino Software 1.6.0 - Intel 1.0.4**

| Operating system | File size | File type |
|---|---|---|
| Linux 32-bit | 140 MB | .tgz |
| Linux 64-bit | 147 MB | .tgz |
| Mac OS X | 229 MB | .zip |
| Windows | 304 MB | .7z |

At the time of writing, the latest version available was 1.6.0. After the software has been downloaded, simply install it using the onscreen instructions, depending on your operating system.

## How to do it...

Once you've downloaded and installed the software, the next step is to connect the board and install the drivers. This process differs for each operating system.

Updating the Galileo firmware is a good first step after the installation of the drivers. It helps verify that your software and drivers are set up correctly, and it prepares your Galileo board with the most up-to-date firmware available. Follow these steps to go through this recipe:

1. Reboot the Galileo board (no SD Cards!). To reboot the Galileo, first *unplug the USB cable*. Then *unplug the 5V adapter* from the board. If there is an SD card in the Galileo, *remove it* before powering the board back up.

   To power the board back up, make sure you plug the *5V cable in first*, then plug a USB cable into the *USB Client* port.

2. The next step is to set up the Arduino Galileo IDE. To do so, open up the Galileo-specific Arduino software you downloaded earlier.

3. Next is serial port selection, which involves two steps:

   ❑ The first step is to select the serial port. Go to the **Tools** menu, then hover over **Serial Port**.

   ❑ Under the **Tools | Board** menu, make sure **Intel Galileo** is selected.

4. The next step is the firmware update process. To update the board firmware, go to **Help | Firmware Update**. Then, click **Yes** to proceed.

The software will attempt to communicate with your board and read the current version of the firmware. In the next window that pops up, select **Yes** to acknowledge that you'd like to upgrade the firmware, and the process will begin.

While the progress bar zooms across your screen, make sure you *don't unplug either the power or the USB cable* from the Galileo. As the popup says, the update procedure will take about five minutes. A `Target Firmware Upgraded Successfully` popup will appear after the update completes.

We can now test the Arduino IDE and upload some basic code to the Galileo board. This is the main window of the IDE:

You can see that I have already loaded the **Blink** example here. You can find it in **Files | Examples | Basic**. We are going to use this sketch just to see if the Arduino IDE is working properly.

Now, you also need to tell the IDE which board you are using. To do this, go to **Tools | Board** and select **Intel Galileo Gen 2**, as shown in the following screenshot:

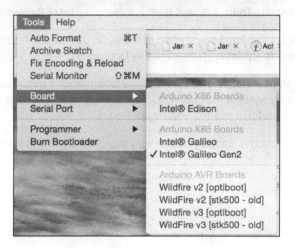

You should also go to **Serial Port** on the **Tools** menu to select the serial port that corresponds to your Galileo board. This is necessary if you have several serial devices connected to your computer, for example other Arduino boards.

Press the **Upload** button to upload the code to your board. You should see that the code has been uploaded in the console of the IDE, and that the onboard LED of the Galileo board starts blinking at regular intervals.

## How it works...

The Intel Galileo is compatible with most of the usual Arduino commands, and can be programmed using a modified version of the Arduino IDE. When you upload code to Intel Galileo, the Intel Galileo processor is actually emulating an Arduino microcontroller, thus providing a transparent experience for the user, who can then use the Galileo board as a classical Arduino board, similar to Arduino Uno.

## See also

This recipe is the foundation for all the remaining recipes in this chapter. Don't hesitate to check out the last recipe of this chapter if you encounter any problems at this stage. You can also check all the characteristics of the Galileo board, such as which pins you can use, on this page on the Arduino website at https://www.arduino.cc/en/ArduinoCertified/ IntelGalileo.

# Connecting an analog sensor

In this recipe, we are going to see how to connect an analog sensor to our Galileo board. Analog sensors are widely used in measurement systems, and can be used to measure a wide range of data such as temperature, light levels, barometric pressure, and so on.

In this recipe, we are going to see how to measure the ambient temperature using an analog temperature sensor.

## Getting ready

For this recipe, apart from the Intel Galileo board, you will need a TMP36 analog temperature sensor.

You will also need a breadboard and a few male/male jumper wires to make the connections between the different components. Note that you will use this breadboard and the wires for most of the recipes in this book.

This is the list of all the extra components you will need for this recipe:

▸ TMP36 sensor (`https://www.sparkfun.com/products/10988`)

▸ Breadboard (`https://www.sparkfun.com/products/12002`)

▸ Jumper wires (`https://www.sparkfun.com/products/9194`)

## How to do it...

The first step is to assemble the hardware for this project. To help you out, this is the corresponding schematic:

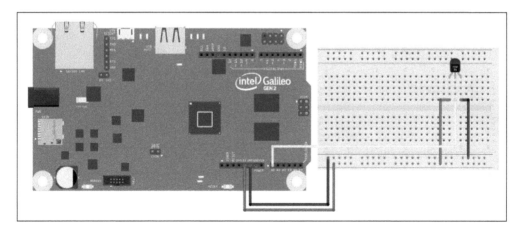

Building the project is quite simple. First, place the TMP36 sensor on the breadboard. Then, connect the power supply from the Galileo board to the breadboard; 5V goes to the red power rail (**+**), and GND to the blue power rail (**-**).

After that, connect the left pin of the sensor (pin 1 of the sensor, as shown in the schematic circuit in the preceding diagram) to the red power rail, and the right pin of the sensor to the blue power rail. Finally, connect the middle pin of the sensor to the analog pin A0 of the Galileo.

This is what it should look like:

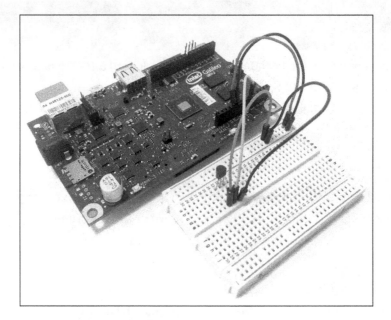

We are now going to program the Galileo board so it measures the temperature and displays it inside the Arduino IDE's serial port. This is the complete code for this part:

```
// Sensor pin
int sensorPin = 0;

void setup()
{

  // Start Serial connection
  Serial.begin(9600);
}

void loop()
{
```

```
// Read data from sensor pin
int reading = analogRead(sensorPin);

// Convert to voltage
float voltage = reading * 5.0;
voltage /= 1024.0;

// Print voltage
Serial.print(voltage); Serial.println(" volts");

// Print temperature
float temperatureC = (voltage - 0.5) * 100 ;
Serial.print(temperatureC); Serial.println(" degrees C");

// Wait a second
delay(1000);

}
```

**Downloading the example code**

You can download the example code files from your account at `http://www.packtpub.com` for all the Packt Publishing books you have purchased. If you purchased this book elsewhere, you can visit `http://www.packtpub.com` and register to have the files e-mailed directly to you.

You can simply paste this code into the Arduino IDE and then upload it to the board. Then, open the serial monitor. The serial monitor is used to display information coming from the board, and we will use it a lot for debugging purposes. You should see that, every second, the measured voltage and the corresponding temperature are displayed on the serial monitor.

## How it works...

The sketch in this recipe continuously measures the voltage on the analog pin A0. We know from the TMP36 sensor datasheet that this voltage is directly linked to the ambient temperature.

Therefore, we first convert the reading from the A0 pin to the corresponding voltage. Then, we convert this value into a useful temperature by using the formula given by the sensor manufacturer.

After that, we simply print this value to the serial monitor so that it can be displayed via the Arduino IDE.

## See also

Later in this chapter, there is a recipe called *Displaying temperature on an LCD screen*, which uses the same sensor and displays the temperature on an LCD screen.

# Connecting a digital sensor

In this recipe, we are going to see how to use a digital sensor with the Intel Galileo board. Digital sensors are also widely used in electronics, from the simple motion sensor that we will use in this recipe, to more complex digital sensors such as the 3-axis digital accelerometers that can be found in smartphones.

## Getting ready

For this recipe we will be using a simple PIR motion sensor. You can find this sensor at `https://www.sparkfun.com/products/8630`.

## How to do it...

We are now going to assemble our project. Just as for previous recipes, first connect the power supply from the Galileo board to the breadboard.

Then, connect the PIR motion sensor to the breadboard. Connect the red wire (the left wire in the schematic, on pin number 1) from the motion sensor to the red power rail, and the black wire (the right wire in the picture) to the blue power rail.

Finally, connect the yellow (signal) wire in the middle of the PIR motion sensor to pin number 7 on the Galileo board. You can use the following schematic to help you out:

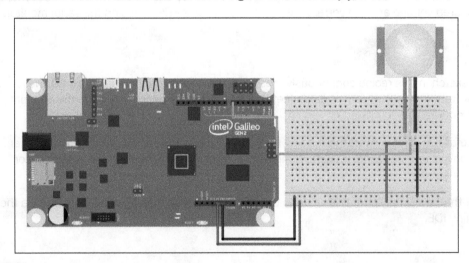

This is the final result (I didn't use a breadboard here and connected the sensor directly to the Galileo):

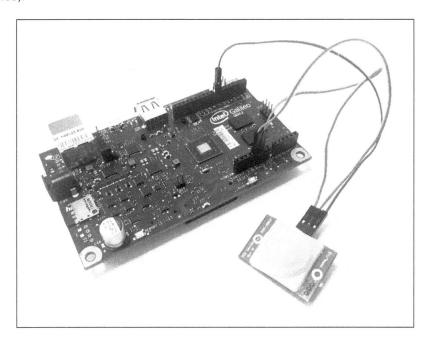

We are now going to program the board to read data from the PIR sensor, and display it on the serial port. This is the complete code for this part:

```
// Sensor pin
int sensorPin = 7;

void setup()
{
  // Start Serial connection
  Serial.begin(9600);
}

void loop()
{

  // Read data from sensor pin
  int reading = digitalRead(sensorPin);

  // Print reading
  Serial.println(reading);
```

```
   // Wait a second
   delay(1000);


}
```

You can simply copy and paste this code into the Arduino IDE. Then, upload it to the Galileo board. You can now open the serial monitor, you should see that for every second, the state of the motion sensor is printed on the serial monitor.

Now, try to pass your hand in front of the sensor, you should see that it turns red, and see the state change instantly inside the serial monitor.

## How it works...

PIR motion sensors are quite simple to use; they basically return a logical state of LOW when they don't detect any motion, and a logical state of HIGH when motion is detected in front of the sensor.

Therefore, in the preceding code, we check the state of the pin to which the sensor is connected every second. Then, we simply display the state of the sensor inside the serial monitor, so that it can be monitored by the user.

## See also

You can now go to the next recipe to learn how the Galileo board can communicate with a more complex digital component, an LCD screen that communicates via the **Inter-Integrated Circuits (I2C)** protocol with the Galileo board.

# Connecting an LCD screen

We are going to connect an LCD screen to the Galileo board in this recipe. This LCD screen will be used to display useful information. In this recipe, we will simply see how to use the LCD screen. We will use an LCD screen that has a built-in I2C interface for this project, as they are really easy to use with the Galileo board.

## Getting ready

For this project, you will need an LCD screen. I used a 4 x 20 lines LCD screen with an I2C interface (a SainSmart I2C LCD screen 4 x 20). You can use a smaller LCD screen, but you really need one with an I2C interface or it won't work. The link to the LCD screen I used for this project is `http://www.sainsmart.com/sainsmart-iic-i2c-twi-serial-2004-20x4-lcd-module-shield-for-arduino-uno-mega-r3.html`.

For the software, you will also need the library to control the I2C LCD screen we are using in this project:

`https://github.com/fdebrabander/Arduino-LiquidCrystal-I2C-library`

To install this library, simply put the downloaded folder into your Arduino libraries folder. Alternatively, you can use the **Sketch | Include** library tool from the Arduino IDE to add the library into the Arduino IDE.

## How to do it...

We are now going to assemble the hardware. Thanks to the I2C interface, it is relatively easy to connect the LCD screen to the Galileo board. The I2C interface is commonly used in such projects, to simplify the connection and communication between devices.

First, connect the power supply to the breadboard as we did in previous recipes. Then, insert the connector from the LCD screen into the breadboard. After that, connect the red cable to the red power line, and the black cable to the blue power line. Then, simply connect the I2C lines (SDA and SCL) to the pins of the same name on the Galileo board.

This is what the assembly should look similar to:

Now, we are going to program the Galileo board via the Arduino IDE to test the LCD screen and print some characters on it. This is the complete code for this part:

```
// Libraries
#include <LiquidCrystal_I2C.h>
#include <Wire.h>

// LCD Screen
LiquidCrystal_I2C lcd(0x27,20,4);

void setup()
{
    // Start Serial connection
    Serial.begin(9600);

    // Init LCD
    initDisplay();

    // Display text
    lcd.print("This is a simple test.");

}

void loop()
{

}

// Init LCD display
void initDisplay()
{
    lcd.init();
    lcd.backlight();
    lcd.clear();
}
```

Now, simply copy this code and paste it inside the Arduino IDE. Then, upload the code to the Arduino board.

You should immediately see that the LCD screen's backlight turns on, and that the LCD displays the test message, `This is a simple test.`

## How it works...

The LCD screen we are using in this recipe uses an I2C interface, which is a very convenient interface to use with the Galileo board. As we saw earlier, it allows us to connect the LCD screen to the Galileo board using only two data wires.

As we saw in the code, it also allows us to easily control the LCD screen with simple commands. For example, only a single line of code is required to turn on the LCD screen's backlight.

It is also very easy to print a message on the LCD screen, as we can use the same `print()` function as with the serial monitor.

## See also

I now recommend looking at the next recipe, as you will learn how to combine two recipes from this chapter, and you will be able to display the temperature readings on the LCD screen.

# Displaying the temperature on an LCD screen

We are now going to see how to combine several of the concepts we learned in the previous recipes. We are going to read data from the same analog temperature sensor we used earlier in this chapter, and display the readings from this sensor on the LCD screen we used in the previous recipe.

## Getting ready

For this project, you will need an LCD screen. I used a 4 x 20 lines LCD screen with an I2C interface. You can use a smaller LCD screen, but you really need one with an I2C interface or it won't work. You will also need a TMP36 temperature sensor.

This is the link for all the parts I used for this recipe:

- SainSmart I2C LCD screen 4 x 20 (`http://www.sainsmart.com/sainsmart-iic-i2c-twi-serial-2004-20x4-lcd-module-shield-for-arduino-uno-mega-r3.html`)
- TMP36 sensor (`https://www.sparkfun.com/products/10988`)

As in the previous recipe, you will also need the I2C display library to control the LCD screen from your Galileo board, which can be found at the following location:

`https://github.com/fdebrabander/Arduino-LiquidCrystal-I2C-library`

To install this library, simply put the downloaded folder into your Arduino libraries folder.

## How to do it...

Let's see how to configure the project.

The first step is to connect the different bits of hardware. You can refer to the recipes, *Connecting an analog sensor* and *Connecting an LCD screen*, for connection instructions.

This is what it should look like:

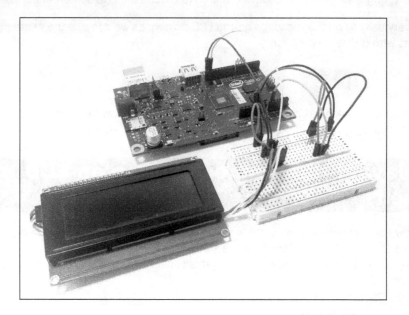

Let's now see how to program the Galileo board for this recipe. This is the complete code for this project:

```
// Libraries
#include <LiquidCrystal_I2C.h>
#include <Wire.h>

// Sensor pin
int sensorPin = 0;

// LCD Screen
LiquidCrystal_I2C lcd(0x27,20,4);

void setup()
{

    // Start Serial connection
```

```
  Serial.begin(9600);

  // Init LCD
  initDisplay();

}

void loop()
{

  // Read data from sensor pin
  int reading = analogRead(sensorPin);

  // Convert to voltage
  float voltage = reading * 5.0;
  voltage /= 1024.0;

  // Print temprature
  float temperatureC = (voltage - 0.5) * 100 ;
  lcd.clear();
  lcd.print("Temperature: ");
  lcd.print(temperatureC);
  lcd.print(" C");

  // Wait a second
  delay(1000);

}

// Init LCD display
void initDisplay()
{
  lcd.init();
  lcd.backlight();
  lcd.clear();
}
```

You can now simply take all the code, and copy and paste it inside the Arduino IDE. Then, upload the code to your Galileo board. You should see that the temperature readings are displayed on the LCD screen, and are updated every second.

This is the result on the LCD screen:

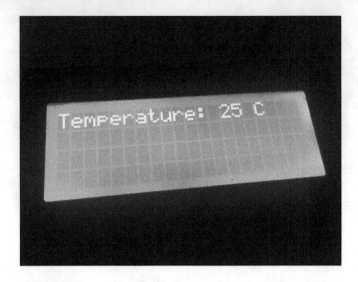

## How it works...

In this recipe, we simply combined the code from the other recipes in the chapter to display the temperature data on the LCD screen.

We start by measuring the temperature data from the sensor, reading the data from the analog pin, and then calculating the temperature from it.

We then display this data on the LCD screen using a series of `print()` commands.

We also repeat this action every second, thereby always updating the temperature readings on the screen.

## See also

You can now use what you learned in this recipe and the other recipes in this chapter to make your own sensor projects using the Galileo board. You can, for example, display data from many sensors measured at the same time on an LCD screen, such as the data from a temperature sensor and a motion sensor.

# Troubleshooting the usual issues with sensors

In this last section of the chapter, we are going to look at the problems you may encounter when connecting sensors to the Galileo board, and how to solve them.

## How to do it...

Some of the common issues include:

- **Uploading a sketch to the Galileo board**: If uploading the code to the board doesn't work, there are several things you can check. First, check that you installed the latest version of the Arduino IDE for the Intel Galileo. Note that it won't work with the normal Arduino IDE.

  Then, check that you selected the correct board inside the Arduino IDE (Galileo Gen 2) and the correct serial port. To be sure that you have the right serial port, make sure you don't have any other serial devices connected to your computer.

  If it still doesn't work, you can also check the official Getting Started guide at `https://software.intel.com/en-us/articles/intel-galileo-board-assembly`.

- **The temperature sensor is returning abnormal readings**: It can happen that the temperature sensor returns abnormal readings such as temperatures that are way too high or way too low. This may be due to the analog nature of the sensor.

  First, make sure that all the wires are correctly connected just as in the relevant recipe. Then, use as short a wire as possible to connect the sensor to the analog pin on the Galileo board, as it will reduce the noise on the sensor.

- **The motion sensor is not working properly**: If you have problems with the motion sensor, the first thing to check is if all the wires have been connected correctly. The sensor should turn red when motion is detected. If this is not the case, and you are sure that all wires were correctly connected, then there might be a hardware problem with the sensor and you will have to replace it.

- **The LCD screen is not displaying any information**: The first thing is to make sure that you wired the LCD screen correctly. Make sure that the SDA and SCL pins are correctly connected to the Galileo board.

  Also make sure that you are using the correct Arduino library if you are using a different LCD screen to the one in the recipe. Also make sure you added the library to the Arduino IDE correctly.

- **The LCD screen is not displaying temperature readings**: If you are sure that the LCD screen is working, then check the sensor individually. There might be a problem with the sensor readings, which causes the information to fail to display on the screen.

# 3

# Controlling Hardware Devices

In this chapter, we will cover the following recipes:

- ▶ Connecting a relay
- ▶ Connecting a DC motor
- ▶ Connecting an XBee module
- ▶ Controlling a servomotor from a rotating knob
- ▶ Using the SD card reader to log data
- ▶ Troubleshooting the usual issues

## Introduction

The Intel Galileo board can be used to control a wide range of devices, and we will get an overview of these functionalities in this chapter.

We are first going to see how to control simple devices such as a relay and a DC motor. This will allow you to control related devices such as lamps, that can easily be connected to a relay for example. Then, we will see how to add more complex devices to the Galileo board, such as an XBee module that can, for example, be used for home automation applications. We will also see how to couple an input device (a knob) with an output device (a servomotor). Finally, we will see how to use the onboard SD card slot on the Galileo board to write measured data onto an SD card.

# Connecting a relay

In the first recipe of this chapter, we are going to see how to connect a relay to the Galileo board, and how to control it. This can, for example, be used in a home automation project, to control a lamp or another electrical device.

## Getting ready

For this project, we will need a relay. I chose a simple 5V relay from Polulu (the Polulu 5V relay module). Of course, you can use any 5V relay module on the market and it should work just fine. You can get this module at `https://www.pololu.com/product/2480`.

You will also need to have your Galileo board ready to use with the Arduino IDE. Please refer to the first chapter if you haven't done this yet.

## How to do it...

First, we need to assemble the hardware. The relay module only has three pins—VCC, GND, and usually one signal pin called EN (or SIG on some modules).

Connect the VCC pin to the 5V pin on the Galileo board. Then, connect the GND pin to the GND pin on the board. Finally, connect the SIG pin on the relay to pin 7 on the Galileo board.

This is the final result:

Let's now write the code for this. This is the complete code for this recipe:

```
// Pin
int relayPin = 7;

void setup() {

  // Pins mode
  pinMode(relayPin, OUTPUT);

}

void loop() {

  // Set the relay active
  digitalWrite(relayPin, HIGH);

  // Wait 5 seconds
  delay(5000);

  // Set the relay active
  digitalWrite(relayPin, LOW);

  // Wait 5 seconds
  delay(5000);

}
```

This code will switch the relay on, wait for five seconds, and then switch it off again. Then, this loop repeats every five seconds.

You can now simply copy this code and paste it inside the Arduino IDE. Make sure that the Galileo Gen 2 board is selected, and that you have selected the correct serial port. Then, upload the code to the board.

You should hear the relay switch turn on and off every five seconds, meaning that you can effectively control a relay from the Galileo board.

## How it works...

The sketch we use in this recipe is really simple. We first define the pin, to which the relay is connected, as an output.

Then, we use the digitalWrite() function to control the state of the relay.

You can now look at the following recipes in this chapter to learn how to control different output devices.

# Connecting a DC motor

We are now going to see how to control a DC motor from the Galileo board. This is slightly more complex than controlling a relay, as we will need to control both the speed and the direction of the motor. To simplify things, we will use a dedicated component (mounted on an Arduino shield) to control the motor.

## Getting ready

For this recipe, we will need two extra components—a DC motor, and an Arduino motor shield.

For the motor, I used a small 5V DC motor. Most 5V motors will work for this recipe.

For the motor shield, I used the official Arduino DC motor shield. However, most shields dedicated to DC motor control will also work for this application. You can, for example, use the SparkFun or DFRobot shields.

This is a list of the components that were used in this project:

▶ Arduino Motor Shield (http://arduino.cc/en/Main/ArduinoMotorShieldR3)
▶ 5V DC motor (https://www.sparkfun.com/products/11696)

You will also need to have your Galileo board ready to use with the Arduino IDE. Please refer to the first chapter if you haven't done this yet.

## How to do it...

Assembling the hardware for this project is really simple. This is a schematic to help you out:

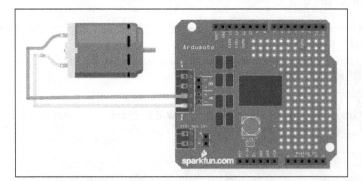

Basically, you need to connect one wire from the motor to a motor shield pin called M+ or M1+ (if there are two motors supported). Then, connect the other pin to M- or M1-. The direction doesn't actually matter here, as we just want to test our motor.

First, put the shield on the Galileo board. Then, simply connect the DC motor to one of the shield's output headers.

This is a picture of the assembled hardware for this recipe:

You will notice that I used a motor shield that is slightly different (another brand) from the one in the schematic, but it works just fine.

This is the complete Arduino sketch for this recipe:

```
// Motor pins
int speed_motor_pin = 6;   // PWM pin
int direction_motor_pin = 7;

void setup(void)
{


}

void loop() {

    // Full speed forward
    send_motor_command(speed_motor_pin,direction_motor_pin,255,1);

    // Wait 5 seconds
```

```
    delay(5000);

    // Full speed backward
    send_motor_command(speed_motor_pin,direction_motor_pin,255,0);

    // Wait 5 seconds
    delay(5000);

}

    // Function to command a given motor of the robot
    // First parameter is the pin controlling the speed of the motor,
    then direction pin, then speed itself, and finally direction of
    the motor
    void send_motor_command(int speed_pin, int direction_pin, int pwm,
    boolean dir)
    {
      analogWrite(speed_pin,pwm); // Set PWM control, 0 for stop, and
    255 for maximum speed
      digitalWrite(direction_pin,dir);
    }
```

Note that, depending on the shield you are using, you might have to modify the pin numbers corresponding to your shield.

Now, simply copy the code above and paste it inside your Arduino IDE. Then, upload the code to your Galileo board.

You should see that the DC motor goes at full speed in one direction for five seconds, and then goes backwards for five seconds.

## How it works...

The whole sketch is organized around the `send_motor_command` function. This is used to do two things—set the speed of the motor, and set the direction.

Setting the speed of the motor is done via PWM, so you can set a speed between `0` and `255` using the `analogWrite()` function.

Setting the direction of the motor is easier—you simply set the corresponding pin on the DC motor shield to HIGH or LOW.

## See also

You can also refer to the recipe on controlling a servomotor, which is a DC motor that can be controlled precisely to turn from a given angle.

# Connecting an XBee module

In this recipe we are going to see how to connect an XBee module to the Intel Galileo board. This is really useful when controlling the board remotely from a computer or another XBee-compatible device. This is particularly interesting for home automation applications.

## Getting ready

You will need several components to add the XBee functionalities to your Galileo board.

First, you will need two XBee modules—the first module for the Galileo board, and the second module for your computer. You can use either the Series 1 or 2 modules for this project, the release version is not relevant here. However, if you are planning to have large XBee networks, I recommend using the Series 2 XBee modules.

You can also use the XBee Pro series, if you need a larger communication range.

You will also need an Arduino XBee shield to plug the XBee module into the Galileo board.

Finally, you will need a USB XBee board to connect the XBee module to your computer.

This is the list of all the components that were used in this project:

- XBee Series 1 or 2 module x 2 (`https://www.sparkfun.com/products/11215`)
- Arduino XBee shield (`https://www.sparkfun.com/products/12847`)
- USB XBee explorer module (`https://www.sparkfun.com/products/11812`)

Note that you need the XBee modules to be of the same series for the project to work. Also note that the XBee shield requires a bit of soldering to make it work.

You will also need to have your Galileo board ready to use with the Arduino IDE. Please refer to *Chapter 1, Installing and Configuring Linux*, if you haven't done this yet.

## How to do it...

It's now time to assemble the project. This is really simple. First, plug the XBee Arduino shield into the Galileo board. Then, simply plug one XBee module on top of the shield.

For the computer module, plug the other module into the XBee USB explorer board, and then connect the board to your computer with a USB cable.

This is the result, with the XBee module plugged into the Galileo board:

This is the complete code for this recipe:

```
void setup() {

  // Start serial
  Serial1.begin(9600);
  Serial.begin(9600);

}

void loop() {

  // Check for Serial data
  if (Serial1.available()) {

    // Read one byte
    char c = Serial1.read();

    // Echo the value that was read on Serial1 & Serial
    Serial.print(c);

  }
}
```

This code is basically an `echo` code that sends back any character that is sent to the board via the serial port or the XBee module. Here, we need to use the `Serial1` object to make sure we are talking to the XBee module on the Galileo board.

We will, for example, send a message from the USB XBee module connected to our computer, and see it arrive on the Galileo board and back.

You can now copy this code and paste it inside the Arduino IDE. After that, open the Arduino IDE's serial monitor.

Make sure that the serial monitor is set to a speed of `9600`, and then select the serial port corresponding to the XBee USB Explorer board. All these configuration options are shown in the serial monitor window.

Then, simply type a message in the serial monitor, for example `Hello`. You should see that the same message is printed back on the serial monitor, meaning that the message went to the board, and was then sent back via XBee to our computer. This is because, by default, the XBee modules are configured to be on the same network and talk to every other XBee module in the network.

To get more configuration options for your XBee modules, you can also get the official X-CTU software here:

```
http://knowledge.digi.com/articles/Knowledge_Base_Article/X-CTU-XCTU-
software
```

## How it works...

In this project, the XBee modules act as a serial port over the air. We wrote an Arduino code sketch that echoes any incoming data on the serial port. This will also work with the USB cable that we used to program the Galileo board.

However, we can now communicate directly with the board via XBee because we set the switch on the XBee board so that the Galileo board serial port is directly connected to the XBee module.

## See also

You can use what you learned in this recipe and mix it with the other recipes in this chapter, for example, to control a relay wirelessly via XBee.

# Controlling a servomotor from a rotating knob

We are now going to link an input component (a rotating knob) with an output, in this case a servomotor. A servomotor is a DC motor which has extra components so that it can be controlled precisely. You can, for example, order it to turn at a given angle. We will write some code so that, when the knob is turned, the servomotor will turn instantly as well.

## Getting ready

You will need two extra components for this project—a servomotor and a rotating knob.

I used a standard 5V servomotor for this recipe, and most brands will work for this project. It just needs to be rated at 5V. I also used a small 10k rotating potentiometer to act as the rotating knob.

This is a list of all the extra components that I used for this project:

▶ A rotating potentiometer with knob (`https://www.sparkfun.com/products/9806`)

▶ A servomotor (`https://www.sparkfun.com/products/9065`)

Note that, usually, servomotors come with a 3-pin female header that is difficult to connect to a breadboard. You might need a 3-pin female-to-male adapter to connect the servomotor to the breadboard.

You will also need to have your Galileo board ready to use with the Arduino IDE. Please refer to the first chapter if you haven't done this yet. This is a picture of the rotating knob that I used for this project:

And this is a closer look at the servomotor that was used for this project:

## How to do it...

The first step is to assemble the hardware for this project. Let's start with the servomotor. Connect the servomotor VCC wire (usually red) to the red power rail on the breadboard. Then, connect the servomotor GND wire (usually black) to the blue power rail on the breadboard. Finally, connect the signal wire to pin number 9 on the Galileo board. It is necessary here to connect the signal wire to a PWM pin as we can use this pin to change the angle of the servo motor. A simple digital pin will not work for this application.

Then, connect the rotary knob to the breadboard. Connect the middle pin to pin A0 on the Galileo board. Then, connect one of the other pins to the red power rail, and another one to the blue power rail.

Finally, connect the power supply—connect the 5V pin to the red power rail, and the GND pin to the blue power rail. This is the final result with the servomotor and the rotary knob connected to the Galileo board:

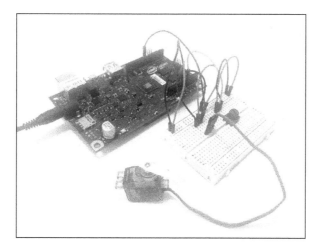

This is the code that we used to control the servomotor via the rotary knob:

```
// Code to control the servomotor via a potentiometer
#include <Servo.h>

// Pins
int potPin = A0;

// Servo object
Servo myservo;


void setup() {


  // Pins mode
  pinMode(potPin, INPUT);

  // Attach servo
  myservo.attach(9);

}
void loop() {

  // Read data from potentiometer
  float reading = analogRead(potPin);
  float servo_position = reading/1024. * 180.;

  // Change servo position
  myservo.write(servo_position);
}
```

You can now copy this code and paste it inside the Arduino IDE. Then, upload it to the board.

You can now test the project. Turn the rotary knob, and you should see that the servomotor turns as well. You should see that the potentiometer turns at an angle which is proportional to the angle of the knob.

## How it works...

This code uses the Arduino IDE `Servo` library which makes it really easy to control servomotors. The code's functionality is also really simple. At every iteration of the Arduino loop, we first measure the value from the rotary knob by using the `analogRead()` function.

Then, we convert this value into an angle. We know that there are 1,024 possible values for this reading, and that the servo servomotor can turn from 0 to 180 degrees. We then simply convert the analog reading by dividing it by 1,024, and multiplying it by 180.

Finally, we set this angle to the servomotor via the `Servo` library.

## See also

You can also apply what you learned in this chapter to control other devices, such as the relay or the DC motor that we learned how to use in the initial recipes of this chapter.

# Using the SD card reader to log data

In the last recipe of the chapter, we are going to see how to use a device that is already integrated with the Intel Galileo board: the SD card reader. We will see how to use it to log data measured by the Galileo board.

## Getting ready

For this project, you will need two extra components along with the Galileo board. You will first need a micro SD card to log data using the SD card reader. If you followed the recipes in the previous chapter, you should already have an SD card on your Intel Galileo board.

I also used a simple TMP36 temperature sensor to get some data to log on the SD card.

This is the list of the extra components that were used in this project:

- ▶ Micro SD card (`https://www.sparkfun.com/products/11609`)
- ▶ TMP36 sensor (`https://www.sparkfun.com/products/10988`)

You will also need to have your Galileo board ready to use with the Arduino IDE. Please refer to the first chapter if you haven't done this yet. This is a close-up picture of the SD card that was inserted into the Galileo board:

## How to do it...

The hardware configuration for this project is really simple. First, insert the micro SD card into the SD card slot, if you haven't done that yet.

Then, plug in the TMP36 sensor, as shown in the following picture:

Then, connect the left pin to the Galileo 5V pin, the middle pin of the sensor to the Galileo AO pin, and the right pin of the sensor to the GND pin on the board. To see where the pins are on the sensor, refer to the preceding picture.

This is now the complete code for this recipe:

```
// Libraries
#include <SD.h>

// Sensor pin
int sensorPin = 0;

// For SD card
const int chipSelect = 4;

void setup()
{

  // Start Serial connection
  Serial.begin(9600);
  // Init SD card
  Serial.print("Initializing SD card...");

  // See if the card is present and can be initialized:
  if (!SD.begin(chipSelect)) {
    Serial.println("Card failed, or not present");
    // don't do anything more:
    return;
  }
  Serial.println("Card initialized.");

}

void loop()
{

  // Make a string for assembling the data to log:
  String dataString = "";

  // Read data from sensor pin
  int reading = analogRead(sensorPin);

  // Convert to voltage
  float voltage = reading * 5.0;
```

```
    voltage /= 1024.0;

    // Print temprature
    int temperatureC = (voltage - 0.5) * 100;
    dataString += String(temperatureC);

    // Open file on SD card
    File dataFile = SD.open("datalog.txt", FILE_WRITE);

    // If the file is available, write to it:
     if (dataFile) {
       dataFile.println(dataString);
       dataFile.close();
       // print to the serial port too:
       Serial.println(dataString);
     }
     // if the file isn't open, pop up an error:
     else {
       Serial.println("Error opening datalog.txt");
     }
    // Wait 10 seconds
    delay(1000);

  }
```

You can now copy this code and paste it inside the Arduino IDE. Then, upload it to the board. After that, open the serial monitor, you should see confirmation messages that the data is being logged every 10 seconds.

You can also power down Galileo at some point, remove the SD card from Galileo, and then insert it into your computer via an adapter. You can then open the `datalog.txt` file, and you should see one line per measurement written in the file.

## How it works...

The code is based on the powerful SD library that comes with the Arduino IDE. We initialize the SD card with the `setup()` function.

Then, at every iteration of the `loop()` function, we build a `String` that will contain the measurement from the temperature sensor. We also check the status of the memory card and the TXT file stored on it.

We also read the temperature value from the sensor using a simple `analogRead()` function. We then convert this reading to a usable temperature. If you need to know more about this, you can look in the corresponding recipe in the previous chapter.

We then use the SD library to open a file called `datalog.txt`. Then, we write a line inside this file that contains the data that was just measured. Finally, we close the file, and we repeat the process every 10 seconds.

## See also

You can use what you learned in this recipe to log more data than just the temperature. Refer to the previous chapter for more examples on how to connect sensors to the Galileo board.

# Troubleshooting the usual issues

There may be issues with all the recipes in this chapter. In this last section of the chapter, we are going to look at the most common issues that can arise with hardware devices and also how to solve them.

## The relay doesn't change its state when the sketch is loaded to the board

If you correctly loaded the sketch, this is most probably a connection problem between the relay and the board, so check the connections first.

Then, also check that the relay is working correctly. To do that, disconnect the signal pin from the Galileo board, and connect it directly to the 5V pin on the Galileo board. Use a breadboard if needed. If the relay doesn't turn on, it means that you have a defective relay that needs to be changed.

## The DC motor doesn't turn when the sketch is loaded to the board

First, check all the connections, and check that you correctly defined the pins to which the motor shield is connected. Check the manufacturer's documentation, if necessary.

Then, also check that the motor itself is working. To do that, just connect the two motor wires directly between the 5V and GND pins of the Galileo board. If the motor doesn't rotate when connected like this, it needs to be changed.

## I can't communicate with Galileo via XBee

If you assembled the XBee modules correctly but you can't communicate with the Galileo board (for example, if you don't have an echo from the board), there are several things you can check.

First, check that the switch on the XBee shield is correctly set to *UART*. This will ensure that the XBee module is directly wired to the serial pins on the Galileo board.

Then, you can also check that the XBee modules are working individually. You can do so by using the XBee software from Digikey, called XCTU, which can be downloaded from the following location:

```
http://www.digi.com/products/wireless-wired-embedded-solutions/
zigbee-rf-modules/xctu
```

Use this software by placing each XBee module into the XBee explorer module, and then check if the software detects it. If not, you might have a defective XBee module. Also check that both XBee modules are in range (put them next to each other, for example).

## The servomotor doesn't turn when the knob is turned

If you turn the rotary knob, there are two things you can check.

You can first check that the knob is working on its own. To do so, create a special sketch where you simply read data from the knob and print it on the serial port. If you see that the data from the knob doesn't change when you turn it, you might have a problem with the connections between the knob and the Galileo board.

Then, you can also check the servomotor separately. Simply remove all the code concerning the knob from the code for this recipe, and see if you can make the servo turn at a given angle by hardcoding the value. If that doesn't work and the connections are correct, you might need to change the servomotor.

## I can't write data to the SD file

If no data is written on the SD card, or you get an error message in the serial monitor, it is most probably a formatting problem. Download the following software from here:

```
https://www.sdcard.org/downloads/formatter_4/
```

Then, use this software to format the card again, and it should work fine.

# 4
# Creating a Web Server

In this chapter, we will cover the following recipes:

- ▶ Using the Intel XDK software
- ▶ Running a simple Node.js server
- ▶ Using Express on Galileo
- ▶ Reading pins via a web server
- ▶ Controlling pins via a web server
- ▶ Creating an API to control Galileo
- ▶ Troubleshooting web server issues

## Introduction

This chapter is an introduction to one of the most important areas of applications on the Galileo board—running a web server. It is relatively easy to run a web server on the board because the Galileo processor runs a simple Linux distribution. This opens the door to a wide range of applications, from simply reading the state of sensors remotely to building bigger web applications based on Galileo.

In this chapter, we will see how to create a basic web server using the Node.js framework along with the Intel XDK software. The combination of these two make things much easier and we will see that it's really simple to run a web server on the Galileo board.

# Using the Intel XDK software

In the first recipe of this chapter, we are going to see how to use the XDK software. XDK was created by Intel to create apps on the Galileo board by using the Node.js framework. You won't have to use any terminal or command lines; everything is done from the XDK graphical interface.

## Getting ready

The first thing to do is get the XDK software. If you need to download it, you can get it from the following link:

```
https://software.intel.com/en-us/html5/xdk-iot#download
```

Then, simply install it by following the onscreen instructions, and then open the software. If this is the first time you have used XDK, you will also be prompted to create an account.

You should see a window similar to this:

Your Galileo board should already be up and running with the Intel IoT image, and connected to your local network. If you cannot see your board at this point inside the XDK interface, just create a new blank project and it should trigger the board discovery process.

## How to do it...

We are now going to connect XDK to your Galileo board. Note that Bonjour needs to be installed on your computer. To do this, select your board next to the **IoT Device** label, as shown in this screenshot:

After clicking on your board, a menu will pop up, asking you to confirm the board's IP address. Add `root` as the username in this window, and then click on **Connect**, as shown here:

After a few seconds, the board and XDK will be connected, and you will get a confirmation message in the XDK console, as shown in this screenshot:

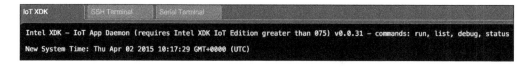

If you can see this message, congratulations, you are now ready to use XDK to program your board!

## How it works...

Intel XDK works with the Galileo board to use Node.js on the board. Node.js is a very powerful framework for developing server-side applications with JavaScript. It makes it really easy to develop complex applications on the Galileo board.

This works by having a daemon (simple software that runs in the background) on the Galileo board that helps communication between XDK and the board. This makes it really easy to write code in XDK and then upload it to the board.

## See also

The next recipe will help you use this to run your first web server on the Galileo board.

# Running a simple Node.js server

In this recipe, we are going to use Intel XDK and Node.js to run a simple web server on the Galileo board. Node.js is a server-side framework written in JavaScript, which is widely used around the world for server applications. Luckily for us, the Galileo board is powerful enough to run Node.js applications, and this is what we will do in this recipe.

## Getting ready

Before we can code our server, we need to create a new project or application in the Intel XDK software. This will allow us to write code inside XDK and upload it to the board. Since we will write all the code from scratch, we can create a blank project, as shown here:

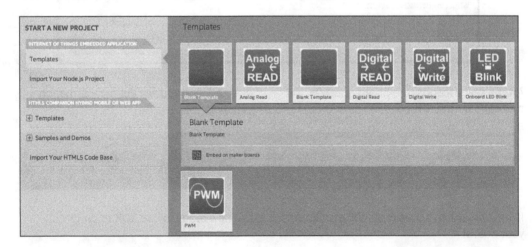

## How to do it...

We are now going to run a simple web server on the Galileo board. This simple server will always answer **Hello World** when we send a request to it. This is the complete code for this recipe:

```
// Required modules
var http = require('http');

// Configure our HTTP server to respond with Hello World to all
requests.
var server = http.createServer(function (request, response) {
  response.writeHead(200, {"Content-Type": "text/plain"});
  response.end("Hello World\n");
});

// Listen on port 3000
server.listen(3000);

// Put a message on the console
console.log("Server started!");
```

You can now simply copy this code and paste it inside the blank project in the Intel XDK. Then, click on the **Upload** button on the bottom toolbar to upload the code to the board. Then, click on the **Run** button, which is near the **Upload** button. This will start the program on the board.

You should see the message—**Server started!** in the console. After that, open your favorite browser, and enter the IP address of the Galileo board, followed by :3000. In your browser, you should see the **Hello world** answer from the server.

## How it works...

The Node.js framework has a module called http, used in this recipe. Using this module, we created a server on our Galileo board. Then, inside the code, we checked for requests coming to the board (for example, from your web browser). Then, at each request, we simply answered with the **Hello world** message.

After that, we simply start the server on port 3000, and print a message inside the console.

## See also

You should now go to the next recipe to discover a new way to create a web server by using the Express framework.

# Using Express on Galileo

In the previous recipe, we saw how to build a minimal web server on the Galileo board, using the Node.js framework. However, it would be really hard to build more complex applications using this; the code would really get complicated.

To handle more complexity, we will use one of the most popular Node.js modules, Express, which also works on the Galileo board.

## Getting ready

Express is a Node.js module that simplifies the process of creating and running web server applications on top of Node.js. You can find more information about Express on the official website at `http://expressjs.com/`.

You don't need to download or modify anything at this point, as Intel XDK will automatically install the Express module.

## How to do it...

We will now see the code to run a simple web server using Express. This is the complete code for this recipe:

```javascript
// Required modules
var express = require('express');
var app = express();

// Main route
app.get('/', function (req, res) {
  res.send('Hello World!');
});

// Start server
var server = app.listen(3000, function () {

  var host = server.address().address;
  var port = server.address().port;

  console.log('Example app listening at http://%s:%s', host,
port);

});
```

You can now copy this code and paste it inside a new Intel XDK project. You should also now modify the `package.json` file in your project. This file is used by XDK to see which modules need to be installed for the current project. This is the content of the file for this project:

```
{
    "name": "blankProject",
    "description": "",
    "version": "0.0.0",
    "main": "main.js",
    "engines": {
        "node": ">=0.10.0"
    },
    "dependencies": {
        "express":"latest"
    }
}
```

As you can see here, we define that we will use the latest version of the Express module.

You can now upload the code to the board again using the same **Upload** button as in the previous recipe. Now, you need to click on the **Build** button in the bottom toolbar because we need to get and install the Express module. This will install the Express module on the board.

When this is done, you can run the application again by clicking on the appropriate button. You will then see the `Example app listening at …` message in the console. After that, open your favorite browser, and enter the Galileo board's IP address, followed by `:3000`. You should see in your browser the `Hello world!` message from the server.

## How it works...

As you can see, the code we used in this recipe was much more compact than the code that used the Node.js `http` module.

Express works with routes, which we can define for each path we want to serve with our server. For example, we created a default route for our app with the following code:

```
app.get('/', function (req, res) {
    res.send('Hello World!');
});
```

Even if the functionalities of the server in this recipe are the same as the `http` module, this modular approach allows you to create more complex applications without complicating the code.

You can now move on to the other recipes in this chapter that will show you how to use a web server based on Express to access the board's functionalities.

# Reading pins via a web server

We are now going to see how to use a web server for useful things. For example, we will see here how to use a web server to read the pins of the Galileo board, and then how to display these readings on a web page.

## Getting ready

For this chapter, you won't need to do much with your Galileo board, as we just want to see if we can read the state of a pin from a web server. I simply connected pin number 7 of the Galileo board to the VCC pin, as shown in this picture:

## How to do it...

We are now going to see how to read the state from pin number 7, and display this state on a web page. This is the complete code:

```javascript
// Required modules
var m = require("mraa");
var util = require('util');

var express = require('express');
var app = express();

// Set input on pin 7
var myDigitalPin = new m.Gpio(7);
myDigitalPin.dir(m.DIR_IN);

// Routes
app.get('/read', function (req, res) {
  var myDigitalValue =  myDigitalPin.read();
  res.send("Digital pin 7 value is: " + myDigitalValue);
});

// Start server
var server = app.listen(3000, function () {

  console.log("Express app started!");

});
```

You can now simply copy this code and paste it inside a blank Node.js project. Also make sure that the `package.json` file includes the Express module.

Then, as usual, upload, build, and run the application using Intel XDK. You should see the confirmation message inside the XDK console.

Then, use a browser to access your board on port `3000`, at the `/read` route. You should see the following message, which is the reading from pin number 7:

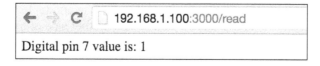

If you can see this, congratulations, you can now read the state of the pins on your board, and display this on your web server!

## How it works...

In this recipe, we combined two things that we saw in previous recipes. We again used the `mraa` module to read from pins, here from pin number 7 of the board. You can find out more about the `mraa` module at:

`https://github.com/intel-iot-devkit/mraa`

Then, we combined this with a web server using the Express framework, and we defined a new route called `/read` that reads the state of the pin, and sends it back so that it can be displayed inside a web browser, with this code:

```
app.get('/read', function (req, res) {
  var myDigitalValue =  myDigitalPin.read();
  res.send("Digital pin 7 value is: " + myDigitalValue);
});
```

## See also

You can now check the next recipe to see how to control a pin from the Node.js server running on the Galileo board.

# Controlling pins via a web server

In this recipe, we are going to do the reverse of what we did in the previous recipe. Here, we are going to see how to control a pin from a Node.js server, just by typing a command into your browser. Let's start!

## Getting ready

The hardware configuration for this recipe is relatively simple, as we just want to check that we can change the state of a pin from a Node.js server.

We will test this with a simple LED and a 220 ohm resistor. You will also need a breadboard and some male/male jumper wires.

To connect the LED to the Galileo board, first place the LED and the resistor in series on the breadboard, by connecting the longest side of the LED (the anode) to the resistor. Then, connect the other resistor pin to the Galileo pin 7, and the other side of the LED (the cathode) to the ground.

This is the final result:

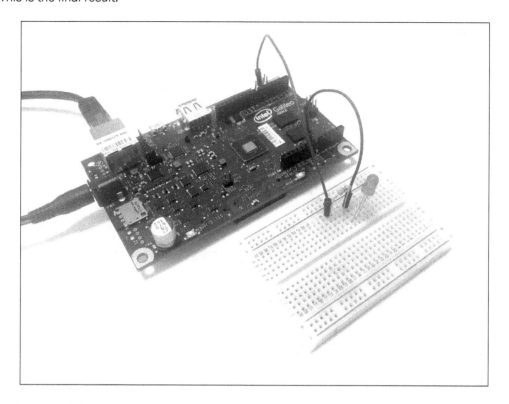

## How to do it...

We are now going to build a simple web server, again based on Node.js and Express, to control this LED by typing simple commands into your web browser. This is the complete code:

```
// Required modules
var m = require("mraa");
var util = require('util');

var express = require('express');
var app = express();

// Set output on pin 7
var myDigitalPin = new m.Gpio(7);
myDigitalPin.dir(m.DIR_OUT);

// Routes
```

```
app.get('/on', function (req, res) {
  myDigitalPin.write(1);
  res.send('Pin 7 is on');
});

app.get('/off', function (req, res) {
  myDigitalPin.write(0);
  res.send('Pin 7 is off');
});

// Start server
var server = app.listen(3000, function () {
  console.log("Express app started!");

});
```

You can now simply copy this code and paste it inside a blank Node.js project. Also make sure that the `package.json` file includes the Express module.

Then, as usual, upload, build, and run the application using Intel XDK. You should see the confirmation message that the server has started inside the XDK console.

Then, use a browser to access your board on port `3000`, at the `/on` route. You should see the following message in your browser:

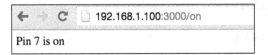

You should also see that the LED is on. To turn it off again, simply do the same but with the `/off` route.

## How it works...

Let's now see how this app works. We used a combination of the `mraa` library to control the pins of the board, and Express to create a web server. We first use the `mraa` library to declare pin `7` as an output, as shown in this line of code:

```
var myDigitalPin = new m.Gpio(7);
myDigitalPin.dir(m.DIR_OUT);
```

Then, we create a server route called /on that sets the state of pin 7 to a HIGH logical state, with this code:

```
app.get('/on', function (req, res) {
  myDigitalPin.write(1);
  res.send('Pin 7 is on');
});
```

We also do something similar with the off state, with this code:

```
app.get('/off', function (req, res) {
  myDigitalPin.write(0);
  res.send('Pin 7 is off');
});
```

## See also

We will now integrate everything we saw in this chapter into a single project. If you want to know more about Node.js modules, you can check out the following link:

```
https://www.npmjs.com/
```

# Creating an API to control Galileo

In the previous recipes, we created a simple web server application to read data from a given pin on the board, or to control a given pin. However, this is not convenient, as you always need to change the code every time you change the pin you want to control.

Here, we are going to learn how to create an API so that you can control any pin on the board from a web browser.

## Getting ready

You don't need anything specific for this recipe, apart from an up-and-running Galileo board with the IoT image, which is connected to your local network.

## How to do it...

In this recipe, we are going to define an API for our Galileo board that will allow us to control any pin on the board, just from a web browser. This is the complete code:

```
// Required modules
var m = require("mraa");
```

```
var util = require('util');

var express = require('express');
var app = express();

// API routes
app.get('/api/read', function (req, res) {

    // Get pin
    var pin = req.query.pin;

    // Return value
    var myDigitalPin = new m.Gpio(parseInt(pin));
    myDigitalPin.dir(m.DIR_IN);
    var myDigitalValue =  myDigitalPin.read();
    res.json({"pin": pin, "value" : myDigitalValue});

});

app.get('/api/write', function (req, res) {

    // Get pin
    var pin = req.query.pin;
    var value = req.query.value;

    // Return value
    var myDigitalPin = new m.Gpio(parseInt(pin));
    myDigitalPin.dir(m.DIR_OUT);
    myDigitalPin.write(parseInt(value));
    res.json({"pin": pin, "value" : value});
});

// Start server
var server = app.listen(3000, function () {

    console.log("Express app started!");

});
```

You can now simply copy this code and paste it inside a blank Node.js project. Make sure that the `package.json` file includes the Express module.

Then, as usual, upload, build, and run the application using Intel XDK. You should see the confirmation message that the server has started, inside the XDK console.

Then, use a browser to access your board on port `3000`. This time, you will need to use the `/api` route, which we will always use to control the board. For example, you can use the following address to read data from pin number `7` on the board:

```
galileo_ip_address:3000/api/read?pin=7
```

This is the result in a web browser:

```
← → C   192.168.1.100:3000/api/read?pin=7
{"pin":"7","value":1}
```

You could also read any other pin using this command, of course.

Let's now see how to use our API to control the pins on the Galileo board. As we need to give both the pin and the state of the pin, we will pass two parameters here. For example, this is the command to put pin 7 in a HIGH state:

```
galileo_ip_address:3000/api/write?pin=7&value=1
```

This is the result in a web browser:

```
← → C   192.168.1.100:3000/api/write?pin=7&value=1
{"pin":"7","value":"1"}
```

You can, of course, do this for any pin on your board, and set the state that you desire. You now have an API to control your Galileo board remotely!

## How it works...

Let's now see how our API works. Again, the application uses a combination of Express and `mraa` to control the Galileo board pins. It is then structured around two main routes, the first route to read the state of a pin, and the other to set the state of a pin.

Note that we send the data back in the JSON format. This format is widely used because it's human readable, but also because it is easy for other apps to use. Here, we send commands to the application using a web browser, but it could just as well be another application.

This is the code for the reading part:

```
app.get('/api/read', function (req, res) {

    // Get pin
```

```
        var pin = req.query.pin;

        // Return value
        var myDigitalPin = new m.Gpio(parseInt(pin));
        myDigitalPin.dir(m.DIR_IN);
        var myDigitalValue =  myDigitalPin.read();
        res.json({"pin": pin,  "value" : myDigitalValue});

    });
```

Here, we get the pin we want to read via the `req.query` object, which has a field called `pin` (that we transmit via the web browser). We then set the corresponding pin as an input, and then return the state of this pin by using the `res.json()` function.

This is the code for setting the state of a pin:

```
    app.get('/api/write', function (req, res) {

        // Get pin
        var pin = req.query.pin;
        var value = req.query.value;

        // Return value
        var myDigitalPin = new m.Gpio(parseInt(pin));
        myDigitalPin.dir(m.DIR_OUT);
        myDigitalPin.write(parseInt(value));
        res.json({"pin": pin,  "value" : value});
    });

    // Start server
    var server = app.listen(3000, function () {

        var host = server.address().address;
        var port = server.address().port;

        console.log("Express app started!");

    });
```

As we can see, it's quite similar to the route we used before, but here we need to get two parameters from the query—the pin, and the state of this pin. Then, we set this pin as an output, set the desired state, and return a confirmation message.

## See also

Congratulations, now you know how to create an API for your board. You can use what you learned in this recipe and combine it with recipes from previous chapters to create exciting projects!

# Troubleshooting web server issues

The last recipe in this chapter covers the known issues with the web server. The following is the list of commonly identified issues and their solutions:

## Intel XDK doesn't see the Galileo board

If you are looking for your Galileo board inside Intel XDK and it doesn't automatically appear, there are several things you can do. First, make sure that your board is correctly connected to your local network, either via Ethernet or Wi-Fi.

Then, simply reboot the board by using the onboard button labeled **REBOOT**. This should solve the problem in most cases.

Finally, the IoT image installed on the board might have a problem. If so, simply follow the relevant recipe to reinstall the IoT image.

If this still fails, go back to the relevant recipe and try to enter the board's IP address manually.

## The web server doesn't respond

If you ran the server application with no errors, but get an error when trying to access the server, make sure that you entered the right port (for example `3000` for all the recipes in this chapter) right next to the board's IP address. If you don't do that, you will get a server not found error in your web browser.

## The Express module can't be found

If you get an error that Express (or another module) can't be found when running the application, it is probably because you didn't install it on your board.

First, make sure that the required module is present in the `package.json` file. If this is not the case, add it, and then upload the code to the board again.

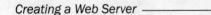

After that, make sure that you clicked on the **Build** button before running the application on the board. Of course, your Galileo board needs to be connected to the Internet to install Node.js modules.

## The Galileo API doesn't work properly

If you are trying the *Creating an API to control Galileo* recipe and it doesn't work properly, first make sure that you are using the correct port to access the API (3000 in the example in this recipe).

Also, make sure that you have entered the correct parameters (such as the pin number and pin state) in the query you send to the API, or it just won't work properly.

# 5

# Hosting Applications on the Galileo Board

In this chapter, we will cover the following recipes:

- ▶ Creating a file-sharing server
- ▶ Accessing weather data remotely
- ▶ Tweeting from the Galileo board
- ▶ Accessing web APIs via Temboo
- ▶ Accessing more APIs via Temboo
- ▶ Troubleshooting hosting issues

## Introduction

In the last chapter, we saw how to host a web server on the Galileo board, and how to use a web server to control our board remotely.

In this chapter, we will build on that and use what we learned to build applications on the Galileo board. We will first see how to use the web server that we created in the previous chapter to create a file-sharing server.

Then, we will use the fact that our board is connected to the Web to learn how to use web **Application Programming Interfaces** (**APIs**) and to interact with web services. We will connect to the Temboo web service to interact with a huge range of APIs. Temboo is a service that makes it really easy to use a wide range of web APIs, without the usual complexity that comes with such projects.

# Creating a file-sharing server

In this first recipe, we are going to see how to create a very basic file-sharing server that can be hosted by the Galileo board. This can later be used as a file-sharing server for your home, or just to include file-sharing capabilities in your applications.

## Getting ready

For this recipe and for the whole chapter, you will need to have your Galileo board running the Intel IoT image, and be connected to the Web via the Ethernet port or the Wi-Fi extension board.

You will also need to have the Intel XDK software installed on your computer.

## How to do it...

The file-sharing server will be really basic here; we will just serve a single file (a video is given as an example). We will again use the Express Node.js framework for this recipe.

This is the complete code for this recipe:

```
// Required libraries
var express = require('express');
var app = express();

// Main route
app.get('/', function (req, res) {
  res.send('Welcome to your fileserver!');
});

// Download route
app.get('/download', function(req, res){
  var file = __dirname + '/upload-folder/dramaticpenguin.MOV';
  res.download(file);
});

// Start server
var server = app.listen(3000, function () {
  console.log('Filesharing server started.');
});
```

You can now just copy this code and paste it into a new Intel XDK project. Of course, if you are modifying the path to your file, you should also modify it in the code. Refer to any recipe in the previous chapter if you need more details on this procedure.

Don't forget to modify the package.json file to specify that we are using the Express framework.

Upload the code to the board, build it, and then execute it. You should immediately see the `Filesharing server started` message in the console.

Then, simply go to the following address from a web server:

```
http://your_galileo_board_ip:3000/download
```

This should immediately start the download of the files to your computer. What we created is a very basic server that allows you to serve files on your network.

## How it works...

Once again, our web server is based on the Express framework, which simplifies things greatly when creating a web server. This time, we used the `res.download()` method to serve files to clients that connect to the server.

The project can, of course, be improved by using a dynamic route in the `app.get()` method, to serve different files depending on their names, transforming this simple example into a real file-sharing server.

## See also

You can now go to the next recipes in this chapter to learn how to interface your Galileo board with web services. Of course, instead of building a file server on your own as we did here, you could have used a ready-made server such as Apache or `lighthttpd`.

## Accessing weather data remotely

In this recipe, we are going to see how to interact with a simple web API—a weather data service called `Forecast.io`. Using this API, we are going to grab the weather data from the service and get it back to our board.

## Getting ready

We need to register with the Forecast.io website, `https://developer.forecast.io/register`, before we can code our project.

The goal is to get an API key that you will find inside your **Account** tab:

Keep this key handy; you will need it soon enough.

## How to do it...

Let's now look at the code. The goal is to connect to the Forecast.io server, send a request to get local weather data, and then print the data inside the console. This is the complete code (this code was taken from the example code in the Forecast.io Node.js module):

```
// Require the module
var Forecast = require('forecast');

// Initialize
var forecast = new Forecast({
  service: 'forecast.io',
  key: 'your_api_key', // Should be replaced with your key
  units: 'celcius', // Only the first letter is parsed
  cache: true,      // Cache API requests?
  ttl: {            // How long to cache requests. Uses syntax
from moment.js: http://momentjs.com/docs/#/durations/creating/
    minutes: 27,
    seconds: 45
  }
});

// Retrieve weather information from coordinates (Sydney,
Australia)
forecast.get([-33.8683, 151.2086], function(err, weather) {
  if(err) return console.dir(err);
  console.dir(weather);
});
```

You can now just copy this code and paste it into a new Intel XDK project. Refer to the previous chapter if you need more details on this procedure.

You need to insert your API key inside the code that you got from the Forecast.io website. Modify the coordinates inside the code for the coordinates of your choice.

Don't forget to modify the `package.json` file, to specify we are using the `forecast` module.

Upload the code to the board, build it, and then execute it. After a while, you should see the weather data in your console:

```
currently:
  { time: 1428574512,
    summary: 'Clear',
    icon: 'clear-night',
```

```
precipIntensity: 0,
precipProbability: 0,
temperature: 22.31,
apparentTemperature: 22.31,
dewPoint: 14.68,
humidity: 0.62,
windSpeed: 5.75,
windBearing: 193,
visibility: 9.99,
cloudCover: 0.2,
pressure: 1021.82,
ozone: 265.84 }
```

If you entered the coordinates of the place where you live, you can check this data against the actual weather to see if it is accurate!

## How it works...

The whole recipe makes use of Forecast.io, which is a free (up to a limit) service to get weather data from all around the globe.

We also used a dedicated module for Node.js, called `forecast`. This greatly simplified the task of interfacing with Forecast.io and getting the data back.

We can also see that the data was sent back to our Galileo board by using a JSON container, which is really useful if we want to use the data in another application.

## See also

I now recommend that you look at the other recipes in this chapter to see how to interact with more web services for the Galileo board.

You could use the information you got from the Forecast.io server and embed this data inside a web page served by the Intel Galileo board.

# Tweeting from the Galileo board

We are now going to see how to send a tweet from the Galileo board. In this recipe, we will see how to interface with Twitter and send a tweet from the board. In the other recipes in the book, you will be able to tweet data measured by your board. To do this, we will interact with the Twitter API.

## Getting ready

Before we can start writing our application, we need to create an account on Twitter, and then an application. To do so, simply go to `https://apps.twitter.com/`.

You will then be able to create a new application, I already had an application from a previous project, as shown in this screenshot:

You will then be able to give a name to your application, as seen in the following screenshot:

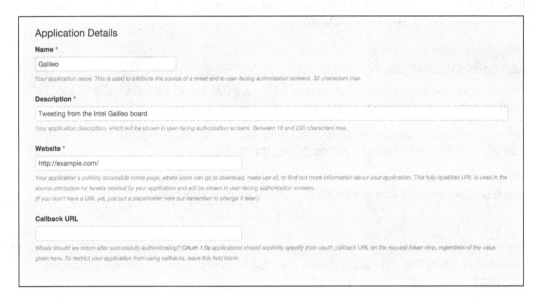

Then, you will get your API key and API secret, which will be useful information for the rest of this recipe:

## Application Settings

*Keep the "Consumer Secret" a secret. This key should never be human-readable in your application.*

| | |
|---|---|
| Consumer Key (API Key) | |
| Consumer Secret (API Secret) | |
| Access Level | Read, write, and direct messages (modify app permissions) |
| Owner | MarcoSchwartz |
| Owner ID | 81862926 |

These keys are linked to the Twitter app you created, and will be used to generate access tokens for your app. On the same page, you will also find your **Access Token** and **Token Secret**, which we will also need for the rest of this tutorial:

## Your Access Token

*This access token can be used to make API requests on your own account's behalf. Do not share your access token secret with anyone.*

| | |
|---|---|
| Access Token | |
| Access Token Secret | |
| Access Level | Read, write, and direct messages |
| Owner | MarcoSchwartz |
| Owner ID | 81862926 |

Finally, we will use a Node.js module called `twit`. Node.js which will install automatically, but you can have a look at it in the GitHub repository:

```
https://github.com/ttezel/twit
```

## How to do it...

We are now going to code the board so it can tweet using the Twitter application we just created. This code will simply post a **Hello World** message on your Twitter account.

This is the complete code (this was taken from the example code in the `twit` Node.js module):

```
// Required module
var Twit = require('twit')

// Twitter data
var T = new Twit({
    consumer_key:          '...' // Your Twitter API key
```

```
    , consumer_secret:         '...' // Twitter API secret
    , access_token:            '...' // Twitter access token
    , access_token_secret:     '...' // Twitter token secret
})

// Tweet
T.post('statuses/update', { status: My First Tweet posted by Intel
Galileo.' }, function(err, data, response) {
  console.log(data);
});
```

You can now just copy this code and paste it into a new Intel XDK project. Refer to the previous chapter if you need more details on this procedure.

You need to enter all your Twitter credentials into the code as well.

Don't forget to modify the `package.json` file, to specify that we are using the `twit` module.

Upload the code to the board, build it, and then execute it.

You should see the `My First Tweet posted by Intel Galileo` message appear on your Twitter account after a few moments. You will also get a confirmation message in the Intel XDK console.

## How it works...

The whole recipe is based on the Node.js `twit` module, which makes it really easy to post tweets from Node.js. Have a look at the module's documentation, you can also use it to read tweets, for example.

## See also

In the next two recipes, we are going to see how to use the Temboo service to easily access many more web APIs.

You can take some more time now to explore the Twitter API. For example, you can also get data from Twitter using your Galileo board, for example, trending topics.

# Accessing web APIs via Temboo

In this recipe we are going to see how to use Temboo, which is a website that sets up the interface between development boards (such as Galileo) and many web services (such as Twitter).

Using Temboo greatly simplifies the use of several web APIs, and it is also free up to a monthly limit of calls to the Temboo service.

We will use Temboo as an example to get the latest mentions or posts on Facebook from the Galileo board.

## Getting ready

Before we can use Temboo, we need to create an account. Simply go to `http://www.temboo.com`.

You should be able to sign up, as shown in the following screenshot:

After you create an account, you will be able to get a list of all the available libraries, which are organized into **CHOREOS**, which are specific pieces of code providing a given function:

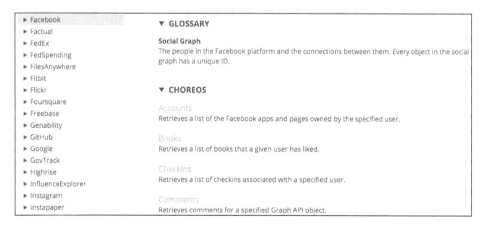

I have selected Facebook for this example, so you can now explore all the Facebook **CHOREOS**.

## How to do it...

Let's now see how to use the Facebook library, and the relevant choreo, to post a message on Facebook. The choreo we will use in our recipe is called **GetLatestMention**:

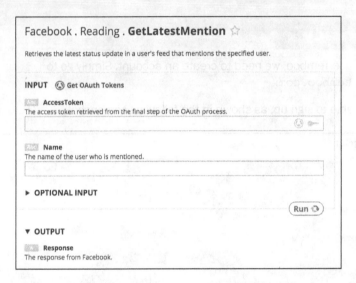

Before we can use this choreo, we need to create a Facebook application. To do this, simply go the web address at `https://developers.facebook.com`.

You will then be given an **App ID** and an **App Secret** that you will need to use on Temboo, as shown in this screenshot:

Then, in the **Site URL**, type the URL shown in the following screenshot:

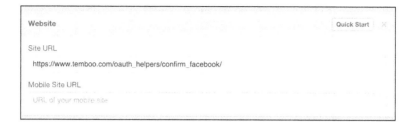

You can now go back to Temboo. Enter your **App ID** and **App Secret** values in these fields:

This will generate an access token, which you will need for the app, as shown here:

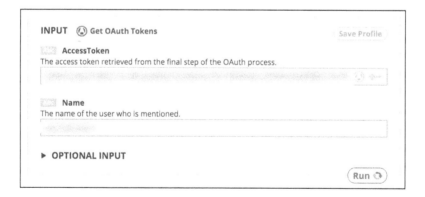

Temboo will then automatically generate some code, based on the data that you entered before:

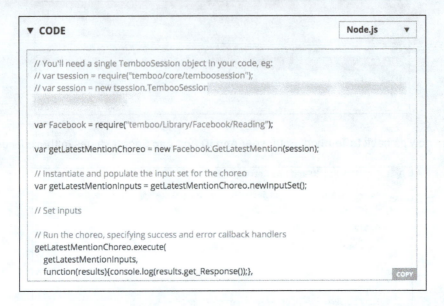

You can also use the code generated from Temboo:

```
// You'll need a single TembooSession object in your code, eg:
var tsession = require("temboo/core/temboosession");
var session = new tsession.TembooSession("your_temboo_name",
"app_name", "app_token");

var Facebook = require("temboo/Library/Facebook/Reading");

var getLatestMentionChoreo = new
Facebook.GetLatestMention(session);

// Instantiate and populate the input set for the choreo
var getLatestMentionInputs = getLatestMentionChoreo.newInputSet();

// Set inputs
getLatestMentionInputs.set_Name("facebook_name");
```

```
getLatestMentionInputs.set_AccessToken("facebook_app_token");

// Run the choreo, specifying success and error callback handlers
getLatestMentionChoreo.execute(
    getLatestMentionInputs,
    function(results){console.log(results.get_Response());},
    function(error){console.log(error.type);
console.log(error.message);}
);
```

You can now just copy this code and paste it into a new Intel XDK project. Refer to the previous chapter if you need more details on this procedure.

You will also need to enter your Temboo name, the app name, and the app token at the start of the code, and also your Facebook app name and the app token, later in the code.

Don't forget to modify the `package.json` file, to specify that we are using the Temboo module.

Upload the code to the board, build it, and then execute it. You should see the last time you were mentioned on Facebook in the console!

## How it works...

This recipe is the perfect example of what Temboo can do for you and your Galileo projects. It simplifies the link between your applications and web APIs such as the Facebook API.

## See also

You can now use Temboo to access many more web APIs, as we will see in the next recipe.

# Accessing more APIs via Temboo

In this recipe, we will see how to access more web APIs, so that we can give even more functionalities to our Galileo projects.

## Getting ready

Follow the section in the previous recipe to see how to create an account on Temboo.

## How to do it...

We are now going to look at some important choreos that should be useful in your Galileo projects.

There is a very good search engine on Temboo using which you can classify choreos by their field of application, as shown in this screenshot:

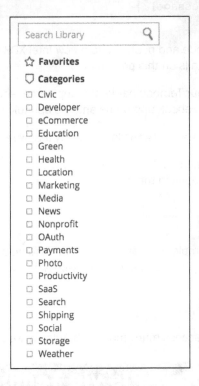

For example, selecting **eCommerce** returns the following output:

If you are reading this book, you are most probably a developer. Therefore, you might be interested in the **GitHub** choreo:

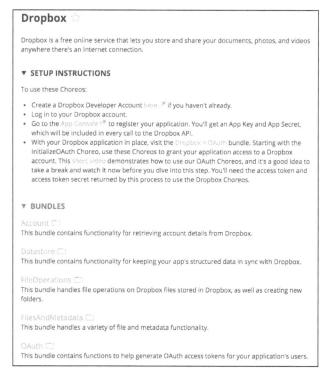

> ## GitHub ☆
>
> GitHub has changed the way code is shared. A web service for development projects, it uses the Git revision source control system (Oh Linus, thank you!), and allows you to share code with friends, co-workers, classmates, and anonymous users.
>
> ### ▼ BUNDLES
>
> GistsAPI ☐
> The Gist API gives developers an easy way to share snippets and pastes with others.
>
> GitDataAPI ☐
> The Git Data API gives you access to read and write Git objects to your Git database on GitHub and to list and update your references such as branch heads and tags.
>
> IssuesAPI ☐
> The Issues API gives developers an easy way to access issues associated with GitHub repositories.
>
> OAuth ☐
> This bundle contains functions to help generate OAuth access tokens for your application's users.
>
> ReposAPI ☐
> The Repos API gives developers an easy way to access GitHub objects such as repos, collaborators, comments, commits, contents, forks, and more.

By using this choreo, you can transform your Galileo board into a system that automatically reports the issues on your own GitHub repositories!

Another useful choreo is the **Dropbox** choreo:

> ## Dropbox ☆
>
> Dropbox is a free online service that lets you store and share your documents, photos, and videos anywhere there's an Internet connection.
>
> ### ▼ SETUP INSTRUCTIONS
>
> To use these Choreos:
>
> - Create a Dropbox Developer Account here ↗ if you haven't already.
> - Log in to your Dropbox account.
> - Go to the App Console ↗ to register your application. You'll get an App Key and App Secret, which will be included in every call to the Dropbox API.
> - With your Dropbox application in place, visit the Dropbox > OAuth bundle. Starting with the initializeOAuth Choreo, use these Choreos to grant your application access to a Dropbox account. This short video demonstrates how to use our OAuth Choreos, and it's a good idea to take a break and watch it now before you dive into this step. You'll need the access token and access token secret returned by this process to use the Dropbox Choreos.
>
> ### ▼ BUNDLES
>
> Account ☐
> This bundle contains functionality for retrieving account details from Dropbox.
>
> Datastore ☐
> This bundle contains functionality for keeping your app's structured data in sync with Dropbox.
>
> FileOperations ☐
> This bundle handles file operations on Dropbox files stored in Dropbox, as well as creating new folders.
>
> FilesAndMetadata ☐
> This bundle handles a variety of file and metadata functionality.
>
> OAuth ☐
> This bundle contains functions to help generate OAuth access tokens for your application's users.

You can store measurement data in a file with this choreo, and automatically back up that file in your usual Dropbox online storage. Note that the basic (free) plan on Temboo is limited in terms of API calls. If you are developing a project that requires a lot of Temboo calls, you might need to upgrade to a paid plan.

Another useful API is Twilio:

---

## Twilio ☆

Telephony for the cloud era, Twilio's platform lets you easily create scalable voice, VoIP, and SMS text-messaging applications.

**▼ SETUP INSTRUCTIONS**

To use the Choreos in this bundle:

- If you don't already have a Twilio account, sign up for one here ⬀.
- Twilio will provide you with an AccountSID number and an authorization token which you can find on your Account Dashboard here ⬀.

**Please note:** If want to test your application using a Twilio Sandbox number, you'll need to send SMS messages to phone numbers that you've verified. You can manage your verified numbers here ⬀.

**▼ BUNDLES**

Accounts ▢
Twilio allows you to create more than one account. You can create subaccounts which are used for segmenting phone numbers and usage data for your customers and controlling access to data. Choreos within this bundle are used for managing your subaccount resources.

Applications ▢
The Choreos within this bundle allows you to manage applications that you've created with Twilio.

AvailablePhoneNumbers ▢
The Choreos within this bundle allows your application to search for incoming local and toll-free phone numbers that are available for you to purchase.

Calls ▢
The Choreos within this bundle allows your application to initiate calls and retrieve information about calls.

---

**Twilio** is a very nice API that allows you to make automated phone calls from the Galileo board via Temboo. You could have the Galileo board at the heart of an alarm system, which will automatically call you in case motion is detected in side your home!

## How it works...

**Temboo** works on the same principle for all choreos—it makes it easy to link applications running on development boards such as the Galileo, and web APIs.

Therefore, it is now easy for you to link your applications to services such as **Dropbox**, **Twilio**, or **GitHub**.

# Troubleshooting application issues

This section will give you some simple instructions on how to solve problems that can arise when using the recipes in this chapter.

## I can't download files from my file-sharing server

If the server is up and running on your Galileo, but you can't download files from the server, it is probably because you misspelled the name of the file in the code (or in the URL if you are using dynamic routes).

Also check that you are accessing the board via the correct port (`3000`, in the example in the recipe).

## I can't access weather data from Forecast.io

If there are no errors in the console but you still can't see the data, the first thing to check is that you inserted the API key into the code correctly.

Make sure that your Internet connection is active on the Galileo board. Galileo may be connected to your local network, but not to the Internet. If so, reboot the board using the onboard button.

You can also use the error message returned by Forecast.io if you want to learn more about the error.

## My tweets from the Galileo don't show up

If there are no errors in your code but no new tweet shows up on your Twitter account, the first thing to check is that you have entered your credentials into the code correctly.

If you then get an error message from Twitter, analyze the message to see where the problem is coming from. It may be from the permissions that you gave to your app.

## I can't access Temboo from the Galileo board

If the code using Temboo is working, but you can't access Temboo, the first thing to do is to check that you entered all the credentials in the code correctly, both the credentials for Temboo and those for the application you are using.

Check that you haven't reached the Temboo API monthly calls limit. If so, you need to either wait, or take out a paid Temboo plan.

# 6

# Local Network Monitoring

In this chapter, we will cover the following recipes:

- ▸ Accessing measured data remotely
- ▸ Logging data in a local database
- ▸ Displaying measurement data stored in a database
- ▸ Live data visualization
- ▸ Troubleshooting the usual issues with sensors

## Introduction

In this chapter, we are going to learn how to monitor the activity of your Galileo board in your local network.

We are first going to learn how to access the data measured by the Galileo board remotely, and then get it on a web server running on your own computer. Then, we will learn how to store this data in a database on your computer.

In the second part of this chapter, we will look at two recipes about visualizing the data that is measured by your Galileo board, in the form of live charts that you can visualize on your computer.

At the end of this chapter, you will also be able to monitor the state of several Galileo boards remotely, creating a complete remote monitoring solution on your computer.

# Accessing measured data remotely

The first step in this chapter is to access the data measured by your Galileo board remotely. In this first recipe of the chapter, we are going to learn how to do that from a web server running on our computer. This server is based on Node.js, which we already used to program our Galileo board, so we won't have to learn a brand new language. Let's dive in!

## Getting ready

Before we start, we need to be sure that the Galileo board is configured correctly. We will use the data from analog pin AO on the board for the measured data. You can, for example, connect a light level sensor or a temperature sensor to this pin. Refer to *Chapter 1, Installing and Configuring Linux*, to learn how to do this.

You also need to have the Galileo API running on your Galileo board to use this recipe. This is the same API that we created in *Chapter 4, Creating a Web Server*. Here is the complete code for that:

```
// Required modules
var m = require("mraa");
var util = require('util');

var express = require('express');
var app = express();

// API routes
app.get('/api/analog/read', function (req, res) {

  // Get pin
  var pin = req.query.pin;

  // Return value
  var myAnalogPin = new m.Aio(parseInt(pin));
  var myAnalogValue =  myAnalogPin.read();
  res.json({"pin": pin, "value" : myAnalogValue });

});


// Start server
var server = app.listen(3000, function () {

  console.log("Express app started!");

});
```

Refer to *Chapter 4*, *Creating a Web Server*, to learn how to run this code on your Galileo and in order to get the API running.

You will also need your Galileo board's IP address. You can find it in the Intel XDK software. Refer to *Chapter 4*, *Creating a Web Server*, if you need additional help in finding your board's IP address.

Finally, you need Node.js installed on your computer. You can get it from the following location:

```
https://nodejs.org/
```

## How to do it...

We are now going to see how to build a server on our computer, which will query the measurements from the Galileo board. Here is the complete code:

```javascript
var express = require('express');
var app = express();
var request = require('request');

app.get('/', function (req, res) {

  // Make request to Galileo server
  request_options = {
  url: 'http://192.168.1.103:3000/api/analog/read?pin=0',
  json: true
  }
  request(request_options, function (error, response, body) {
    if (!error && response.statusCode == 200) {
      // Display results in a nice way
      res.send("The state of pin " + body.pin + " is " +
body.value + ".");
    }
  });

});

var server = app.listen(3000, function () {

  console.log('App started');

});
```

Note that you will have to modify the code with your Galileo board's IP address. Refer to *Chapter 4*, *Creating a Web Server*, to learn how to find your board's IP address.

Put this code in a .js file, and navigate to the folder with a terminal. Then, type this into the terminal:

```
sudo npm install express request
```

If you are using Windows, you can use the Node.js terminal that comes with Node.js, or use terminal software such as PuTTY. Then, type the following command:

```
node app.js
```

Finally, use your web browser to go to:

```
localhost:3000
```

You should see the following:

This is a live reading coming from your Galileo board, using the API running on your Galileo board. Of course, the value itself may be different, especially if you have a sensor connected to pin A0.

## How it works...

This recipes works by running a server on your computer which queries the Galileo board on demand. When asked to do this, the Node.js server on your computer sends a query to the Galileo board API, and then displays the result on a web page.

Here, we used it for a simple command but we could, of course, access any measurements from the Intel Galileo board. Of course, the Galileo board needs to be connected to the same local network as your computer via Ethernet or Wi-Fi.

## See also

You can now move on to the next recipe to learn how to log these measurements in a database.

# Logging data in a local database

In the previous recipe, we saw how to access data on the Galileo board. It would be even better if we could get this data and then store it in a database on your computer, to be processed, sent, or displayed. This is exactly what we are going to do in this recipe.

## Getting ready

To store data on our computer, we are going to use the powerful MongoDB database, which is commonly used with Node.js. You can find more information about MongoDB at `https://www.mongodb.org/`.

To install it on your computer, follow the instructions here:

`https://www.mongodb.org/downloads`

Then, after following the instructions on the MongoDB website, you will be able to run it on your computer from a terminal. If you are using Windows, use a terminal such as PuTTY. This is what you will see:

```
2015-04-21T09:13:27.140+0200 I JOURNAL  [initandlisten] journal dir=/data/db/journal
2015-04-21T09:13:27.142+0200 I JOURNAL  [initandlisten] recover : no journal files present, no recovery needed
2015-04-21T09:13:27.158+0200 I JOURNAL  [durability] Durability thread started
2015-04-21T09:13:27.158+0200 I CONTROL  [initandlisten] MongoDB starting : pid=12936 port=27017 dbpath=/data/db 64-bit host=macbookpro.local
2015-04-21T09:13:27.158+0200 I CONTROL  [initandlisten] ** WARNING: You are running this process as the root user, which is not recommended.
2015-04-21T09:13:27.158+0200 I CONTROL  [initandlisten]
2015-04-21T09:13:27.158+0200 I CONTROL  [initandlisten]
2015-04-21T09:13:27.158+0200 I CONTROL  [initandlisten] ** WARNING: soft rlimits too low. Number of files is 256, should be at least 1000
2015-04-21T09:13:27.158+0200 I CONTROL  [initandlisten] db version v3.0.2
2015-04-21T09:13:27.158+0200 I CONTROL  [initandlisten] git version: nogitversion
2015-04-21T09:13:27.158+0200 I CONTROL  [initandlisten] build info: Darwin yosemitevm.local 14.3.0 Darwin Kernel Version 14.3.0: Mon Mar 23 11:
59:05 PDT 2015; root:xnu-2782.20.48~5/RELEASE_X86_64 x86_64 BOOST_LIB_VERSION=1_49
2015-04-21T09:13:27.158+0200 I CONTROL  [initandlisten] allocator: system
2015-04-21T09:13:27.158+0200 I CONTROL  [initandlisten] options: {}
2015-04-21T09:13:27.159+0200 I JOURNAL  [journal writer] Journal writer thread started
2015-04-21T09:13:27.377+0200 I NETWORK  [initandlisten] waiting for connections on port 27017
```

Once you can see this on your computer, you are ready to use this recipe, as MongoDB is now running on your computer. Do not close this terminal window as you need to have MongoDB running.

## How to do it...

We are now going to see the code that will allow us to write data in the MongoDB database. First, we are going to see some code that gets measurements from the Galileo board and writes it into the database.

This is the whole code:

```
// Libraries
var request = require('request');
var mongoose = require('mongoose');

// Connect to database
mongoose.connect('mongodb://localhost/galileo');

// Measurement model
```

```
var Measurement = mongoose.model('Measurement', { pin: Number,
value: Number, date: Date});

// Prepare request to Galileo server
request_options = {
    url: 'http://192.168.1.103:3000/api/analog/read?pin=0',
    json: true
}

// Make request to Galileo server
request(request_options, function (error, response, body) {
    if (!error && response.statusCode == 200) {

        // Get time
        var currentTime = new Date();

        // Store in database
        var data_point = new Measurement({ pin: parseInt(body.pin),
value: parseInt(body.value), date: currentTime});
        data_point.save(function (err) {
          console.log('Measurement stored in database');
        });
    }
});
```

You need to modify the code to include your board's IP address.

Put this code in a `.js` file, and navigate to the folder with a terminal. Then, type:

**`sudo npm install request mongoose`**

If you are using Windows, use the Node.js terminal or software such as PuTTY. Then, type:

**`node app.js`**

You should then see a new measurement in the terminal, written into the database.

We also want to check what was actually written in the database. This is the code to do that:

```
// Libraries
var request = require('request');
var mongoose = require('mongoose');

// Connect to database
mongoose.connect('mongodb://localhost/galileo');

// Measurement model
```

```
var Measurement = mongoose.model('Measurement', { pin: Number,
value: Number, date: Date});

// Print all measurements in console
Measurement.find({}, function(err, measurements) {
  measurements.forEach(function(measurement) {
    console.log(measurement);
  });
});
```

Here, you don't need to modify anything in the code. Just put this code in a `.js` file, and navigate to the folder with a terminal. Then, type:

**sudo npm install request mongoose**

If you are using Windows, use the Node.js terminal or software such as PuTTY. Then, type:

**node app.js**

You should then see all the measurements in the terminal, as this screenshot shows:

```
{ _id: 55360333b9d6eaee3a94b9c2,
  pin: 0,
  value: 1020,
  date: Tue Apr 21 2015 09:58:43 GMT+0200 (CEST),
  __v: 0 }
{ _id: 55360346cda79cfe3acaf857,
  pin: 0,
  value: 1020,
  date: Tue Apr 21 2015 09:59:02 GMT+0200 (CEST),
  __v: 0 }
```

If you can see these measurements, it means you just learned how to get data from your Galileo board and store it in a database!

## How it works...

In this recipe, we used the MongoDB database to store measurement data from the Galileo board.

This whole recipe is based on the Mongoose Node.js module, which is a very powerful module to access MongoDB from Node.js. You can see the full MongoDB documentation here:

`http://mongoosejs.com/`

In this recipe, we used it to both write and read data from the MongoDB database, by including this module inside our project in the Intel XDK software.

## See also

You can now go to the remaining two recipes in this chapter to learn how to display data stored inside the MongoDB database.

# Displaying measurements stored in a database

In the previous recipes, we saw how to measure data from the Galileo board remotely and how to store this data in a database. Now, we are going to see how to graphically display this data on your computer.

## Getting ready

To display the data graphically, we are going to use a JavaScript library called `highcharts`, which will make the process much easier. You don't have to install anything, but you can have a look at the library at the following location:

```
http://www.highcharts.com/
```

## How to do it...

We are now going to write the Node.js application that will display the content of the database graphically on a web page. The code will be composed of three parts—a file called `app.js` containing the Node.js code, a file called `index.html` that will contain the interface, and finally another JavaScript file that will query the database's measurements and display them graphically.

Here is the code for the `app.js` file:

```javascript
// Libraries
var express = require('express');
var app = express();
var request = require('request');
var mongoose = require('mongoose');
var path = require('path');

// Set public folder
app.use(express.static(__dirname + '/public'));

// Connect to database
```

```
mongoose.connect('mongodb://localhost/galileo');

// Measurement model
var Measurement = mongoose.model('Measurement', { pin: Number,
value: Number, date: Date});

// Get measurements
app.get('/measurements', function (req, res) {

  // Get all measurements
  Measurement.find({}, function(err, measurements) {
  res.json(measurements);
  });
});

// Display chart
app.get('/', function(req,res) {
  res.sendFile(path.join(__dirname + '/index.html'));
});

// Start server
var server = app.listen(3000, function () {

  console.log('App started');

});
```

The HTML file simply calls the required libraries and creates a blank container for our graph:

```
<script
src="http://ajax.googleapis.com/ajax/libs/jquery/1.8.2/jquery.min.
js"></script>
<script src="http://code.highcharts.com/highcharts.js"></script>
<script src="/js/plot.js"></script>

<div id="container" style="width:100%; height:400px;"></div>
```

Finally, this is the JavaScript file that queries the measurements and then creates the highcharts graph:

```
// Get measurements from database
$.get( "/measurements", function( data ) {

  // Format data
  console.log(data);
```

```
    plot_data = [];
    for (var i = 0; i < data.length; i++) {
      plot_data.push(data[i].value);
    }

    // Plot
    $('#container').highcharts({
        title: {
            text: 'Analog Pin A0 Measurements',
            x: -20 //center
        },
        yAxis: {
            title: {
                text: 'Value'
            },
            plotLines: [{
                value: 0,
                width: 1,
                color: '#808080'
            }]
        },
        tooltip: {
            valueSuffix: '°C'
        },
        legend: {
            layout: 'vertical',
            align: 'right',
            verticalAlign: 'middle',
            borderWidth: 0
        },
        series: [{
            name: 'Measurements',
            data: plot_data
        }]
    });

  });
```

Note that you can get all the files from the GitHub repository here:

```
https://github.com/marcoschwartz/galileo-cookbook
```

Put all the files in a folder on your computer, and navigate to the folder with a terminal. Note that it is important to get all the code from GitHub to get the right structure for the files inside the folder. Then, type:

```
sudo npm install express request mongoose path
```

If you are using Windows, use the Node.js terminal or software such as PuTTY. After that, type:

```
node app.js
```

Finally, use your web browser to go to:

```
localhost:3000
```

You should see the following screenshot:

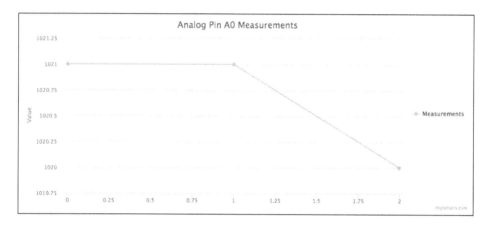

If you can see that, congratulations, you can now display your Galileo board's measurements graphically! As before, your Galileo board needs to be connected to the same local network as your computer, for example, by using the Ethernet port.

## How it works...

This whole recipe is based on the `highcharts` JavaScript library, which makes it really easy to build graphs using JavaScript. This really simplifies the project and makes it very flexible so you can graphically display any kind of data measured by your Galileo board.

## See also

In the next recipe, we are going to work on a flaw in this recipe; it cannot currently display data in real time. We will fix that in the next recipe.

# Live data visualization

In the last recipe of the chapter, we are going to improve the previous recipe by adding a refresh feature to the project, so that the graph is refreshed as new data comes in. This will avoid having to constantly refresh the page.

## Getting ready

Make sure that you have carried out and tested the previous recipe, as we are going to improve it. Of course, as usual, you will find the whole code inside the GitHub repository of the book.

## How to do it...

Here, we are going to improve the code from the previous recipe in order to measure data and display it on the graph.

First, we need to add some code to the app.js file in order to make measurements and write them into the database.

This is done with the following piece of code:

```
app.get('/make_measurement', function (req, res) {

    // Prepare request to Galileo server
    request_options = {
        url: 'http://192.168.1.103:3000/api/analog/read?pin=0',
        json: true
    }

    // Make request to Galileo server
    request(request_options, function (error, response, body) {
        if (!error && response.statusCode == 200) {

            // Get time
            var currentTime = new Date();

            // Store in database
            var data_point = new Measurement({ pin:
parseInt(body.pin), value: parseInt(body.value), date:
currentTime});
            data_point.save(function (err) {
                console.log('Measurement stored in database');
```

```
                res.json({result: 'Measurement stored'});
            });
        }
    });

});
```

Note that you need to modify the code to include your Galileo board's IP address. You can find this IP address in the Intel XDK software.

Then, we need to modify the `plot.js` function so that it constantly measures data, and then display this on a graph.

This is the code:

```
function measure() {

    // Make measurements
    $.get("/make_measurement", function( data ) {

        // Get measurements from database
        $.get( "/measurements", function( data ) {

            // Format data
            console.log(data);
            plot_data = [];
            for (var i = 0; i < data.length; i++) {
                plot_data.push(data[i].value);
            }

            // Plot
            $('#container').highcharts({
                    title: {
                        text: 'Analog Pin A0 Measurements',
                        x: -20 //center
                    },
                    yAxis: {
                        title: {
                            text: 'Value'
                        },
                        plotLines: [{
                            value: 0,
                            width: 1,
                            color: '#808080'
```

```
                              }]
                        },
                        tooltip: {
                             valueSuffix: ' C'
                        },
                        legend: {
                             layout: 'vertical',
                             align: 'right',
                             verticalAlign: 'middle',
                             borderWidth: 0
                        },
                        series: [{
                             name: 'Measurements',
                             data: plot_data
                        }]
                   });

              });

         });

    }

    // Measure every 5 seconds
    measure();
    setInterval(measure, 5000);
```

Note that here we refresh the graph every five seconds, but you can, of course, modify this delay.

On your computer, just grab all the files, such as the HTML files, put them inside a folder, and then navigate to the folder with a terminal. Then, type:

**`sudo npm install express request mongoose path`**

If you are using Windows, use the Node.js terminal or software such as PuTTY. After that, type:

**`node app.js`**

Finally, use your web browser to go to:

```
localhost:3000
```

You should see that the new measurements are displayed on the graph as they are being queried from the Galileo board.

## How it works...

This recipe is a simple improvement on the previous recipe. We are still using the `highcharts.js` library to display the graph.

However, in this recipe, we make new measurements at regular time intervals, and then display these measurements on the graph.

## See also

This is the last recipe in this chapter, so you can now experiment with your own measurements. You can, for example, display several kinds of measurements from the Galileo board on the same graph. You could also display measurements from several Galileo boards on the same graph.

# Troubleshooting the usual issues with sensors

Building local network monitoring applications presents problems as it is a complex topic. Therefore, this section is here to help you out if you encounter problems with your local network monitoring applications.

## I can't get measured data remotely

If you cannot access data remotely from the web server running on your computer, the first thing to check is whether your Galileo board's API is still working, as defined in *Chapter 4, Creating a Web Server*. If necessary, go back to *Chapter 4, Creating a Web Server*, to check exactly how to run the API on your Galileo board.

## Issues with MongoDB

If you have issues with MongoDB, make sure that it was correctly installed. If necessary, follow the advice on the official MongoDB website as the installation instructions change from time to time.

## The graph doesn't appear on the page

If the graph is not being displayed on the page, make sure that you have the latest version of the code from the GitHub repository. You can also use the JavaScript console in your web browser to see if there are any errors on your page. Finally, make sure that the MongoDB database is still running. Also, check the values recorded in the database.

## The graph is not refreshed in real-time

If you were able to see the graph displayed on the web page for the relevant recipe, but it wasn't updated in the last recipe in the chapter, there are many things you can check.

You can, for example, check that the measurement part of the project is working correctly by going back to the first recipe in the chapter. Then, make sure that the data was written correctly in the MongoDB database, by going back to the recipe, *Logging data in a local database*, if necessary.

# 7

# Cloud Data Monitoring

In this chapter, we will cover:

- ▸ Building and testing hardware for cloud monitoring
- ▸ Sending data to a cloud device
- ▸ Monitoring data remotely from a dashboard
- ▸ Logging data in an online datasheet
- ▸ Controlling your board from anywhere in the world
- ▸ Troubleshooting cloud monitoring issues

## Introduction

In this chapter, we are going to continue to build **Internet of Things** (**IoT**) projects with the Galileo board. This time, we are going to see how to monitor data remotely, whether you are at home or on the other side of the world.

To do that, we are going to use different strategies. We are first going to see how to send data to the cloud to be stored online, and then use a dashboard to visualize this data. Then, in another recipe, we will see how to log that data in a spreadsheet. Finally, we will see how to use the MQTT protocol and a dashboard to control your board from anywhere in the world.

## Building and testing hardware for cloud monitoring

In this first recipe, we are going to configure our hardware for cloud monitoring. We are also going to test the project so that we are sure the hardware is working correctly.

---

## Getting ready

You will need a few components for this recipe. First, you will need a TMP36 temperature sensor to be used for temperature measurements. Then, you will need a photocell and a 10k ohm resistor for ambient light level measurements.

This is a list of all the components required for this recipe:

- ▶ TMP36 temperature sensor (`https://www.sparkfun.com/products/10988`)
- ▶ Photocell (`https://www.sparkfun.com/products/9088`)
- ▶ 10k ohm resistor (`https://www.sparkfun.com/products/8374`)
- ▶ Jumper wires (`https://www.sparkfun.com/products/8431`)
- ▶ Breadboard (`https://www.sparkfun.com/products/12002`)

## How to do it...

We are now going to configure the hardware for this recipe. Follow these steps to complete the configuration process:

1. First, we connect the 5V and GND to the top or bottom horizontal rows of the breadboard.

2. Then, we can connect the TMP36 sensor's left pin to the 5V horizontal slot, the middle pin to the analog pin A0, and the right pin to the GND horizontal slot on the breadboard. If you want to see the position of each pin, have a look at the following picture:

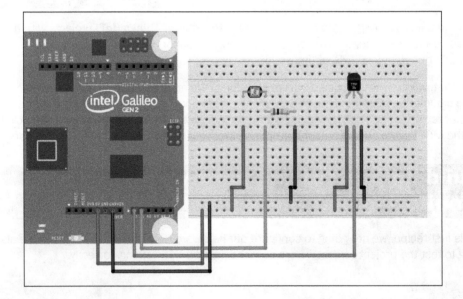

3. Then, position the photocell such that it is in series with the resistor. The node where the photocell and resistor meet should be connected to the board's analog pin A1.

4. Next, connect the free leg of the photocell to the 5V line. The free leg of the resistor should be pinned to the GND.

This is what the hardware configuration looks like when everything is connected:

Once this is done, we are ready to write some simple software to test the components.

## How it works...

We will use two analog sensors in this recipe. Therefore, we are going to use analog `read()` functions to get data from these sensors and print the data in the Intel XDK software console, as a test.

This is the code:

```
// Includes
var mraa = require("mraa");
var util = require('util');

// Sensor pins
var temp_sensor_pin = new mraa.Aio(0);
temp_sensor_pin.setBit(12);
var light_sensor_pin = new mraa.Aio(1);
```

```
light_sensor_pin.setBit(12);
function measure_data() {

    // Measure light
    var a = light_sensor_pin.read();
    var light_level = a/4096*100; // Analog input is on 4096
levels
    light_level = light_level.toPrecision(4);
    console.log("Light level: " + light_level + " %");

    // Measure temperature
    var b = temp_sensor_pin.read();
    var temperature = (b/4096*5000 - 500) / 10;
    temperature = temperature.toPrecision(4);
    console.log("Temperature: " + temperature + " C");
}

// Send data every 10 seconds
measure_data();
setInterval(measure_data, 10000);
```

This code reads data from both analog pins (A0 and A1), converts it into useful data, and then prints it in the console.

As usual, simply copy this code into the `main.js` file in a project in the Intel XDK software, build it, and then run it on the board. This is the result:

```
UPLOADING: Uploading project bundle to IoT device.
[ Upload Complete ]
Intel XDK — Message Received: run
Light level: 77.64 %
Temperature: 25.00 C
```

## See also

You can now move on to the following recipes to see how to send this measured data to the cloud so that it can be monitored remotely.

# Sending data to a cloud device

We are now going to learn how to take measurements from the temperature sensor and the photocell, and send them to the cloud to be logged. They will then be accessible from anywhere, and you will also be able to use them in other applications.

## Getting ready

There is nothing extra you need to do for this recipe. We are going to use dweet.io to store data in the cloud, and you can read more about this service at:

```
http://dweet.io/
```

Dweet.io is a very nice and easy-to-use cloud service for storing data. You make a request to the service with your data, and their servers store it.

## How to do it...

In the project in this recipe, we will take measurements from the sensors, connect to dweet.io, and then send the data to the dweet.io server.

This is the complete code for this recipe:

```
// Includes
var mraa = require("mraa");
var util = require('util');
var request = require('request');

// Sensor pins
var temp_sensor_pin = new mraa.Aio(0);
temp_sensor_pin.setBit(12);
var light_sensor_pin = new mraa.Aio(1);
light_sensor_pin.setBit(12);

function send_data() {

    // Measure light
    var a = light_sensor_pin.read();
    var light_level = a/4096*100;
    light_level = light_level.toPrecision(4);
    console.log("Light level: " + light_level + " %");

    // Measure temperature
    var b = temp_sensor_pin.read();
    var temperature = (b/4096*5000 - 500) / 10;
    temperature = temperature.toPrecision(4);
    console.log("Temperature: " + temperature + " C");

    // Send request
    var device_name = 'galileo_5etr6b'; // Change with your own
name here
```

```
    var dweet_url = 'https://dweet.io/dweet/for/' + device_name +
'?temperature=' + temperature + '&light=' + light_level;
    console.log(dweet_url);

    var options = {
      url: dweet_url,
      json: true
    };

    request(options, function (error, response, body) {
      if (error) {console.log(error);}
      console.log(body);
    });
}


// Send data every 10 seconds
send_data();
setInterval(send_data, 10000);
```

You need to modify something in the code. Dweet.io works on the concept of *things* that identify your device on the cloud. It is labeled as `device_name` in the code sketch, and you should change it to your own name, so that you can identify your own device on the cloud.

You can now just copy this code and paste it in a new Intel XDK project. Refer to the previous chapters, for example, *Chapter 4, Creating a Web Server*, if you need more details on this procedure.

Don't forget to modify the `package.json` file, to specify that we are using the `request` Node.js module.

Upload the code to the board, build it, and then execute it. You should soon see the first set of measurements that were sent to dweet.io:

```
https://dweet.io/dweet/for/galileo_5etr6b?temperature=25&light=84.96
{ this: 'succeeded',
  by: 'dweeting',
  the: 'dweet',
  with:
   { thing: 'galileo_5etr6b',
     created: '2015-04-21T10:26:39.543Z',
     content: { temperature: 25, light: 84.96 } } }

Intel XDK - Message Received: stop
```

## How it works...

The code in this recipe works in a similar way to the code in the previous recipe for measurements. Next, following each measurement, the Galileo board uses the request Node.js module to send a GET request to the dweet.io server, along with the measured data encoded in the URL.

Then, the code reads the answer from dweet.io and prints it in the console.

The whole process is repeated every 10 seconds.

## See also

You should now really see the next recipe to learn how to display this data graphically in an online dashboard.

You can, of course, also experiment with other cloud services that are similar to dweet.io, for example, Xively (https://xively.com/), or Enable IoT (https://dashboard.us.enableiot.com/ui/auth).

# Monitoring data remotely from a dashboard

In this recipe, we are going to build a project on top of what we just created. We are going to use the data that was logged on dweet.io, and display this data in an online dashboard.

## Getting ready

We are going to use a free online dashboard to display the data graphically; Freeboard.io. You can find this at the Freeboard website:

https://www.freeboard.io/

You can now create a new account, and, once this is done, you can create a new dashboard:

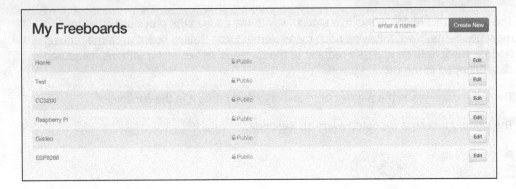

Make sure that the previous recipe, which sends data to dweet.io continuously, is still running.

## How to do it...

We are now going to configure our newly created dashboard so that it can display the measurements from the Galileo board.

The first step is to create a data source that will stream the data into our dashboard. You can do this by clicking on the **ADD** button:

This will take you to a panel where you can fill in the details about your datasource. Basically, you just need to select dweet.io and then enter the NAME of your THING on dweet.io:

Then, you need to link this datasource to a widget that will represent the data graphically. To do that, first add a new **Pane** to your project, and then add a new widget.

There are several widget types available but, for this project, I selected a **Gauge** widget. This is how I filled in the different sections of the `Temperature` widget:

I did the same thing for the light levels; I added another **Pane** and another **Gauge** widget. This is the final result in the dashboard:

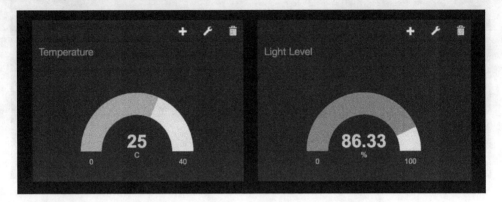

Note that this dashboard can be accessed from anywhere in the world, so you can monitor your Galileo projects from any web browser!

## How it works...

Freeboard.io works by interfacing different data sources (for example, dweet.io) to graphical widgets such as gauges or live graphs. Here, we simply linked the data on dweet.io, generated by the Galileo board, to two widgets on freeboard.io.

## See also

You can now look at the following recipes to learn about other ways to log data online and to monitor the measurements of your Galileo board.

# Logging data in an online datasheet

In this new recipe, we are going to use another way to log data on the cloud; we are going to use a Google Docs spreadsheet to store the data, and then use the built-in functionalities of Google Sheets to plot the data as it arrives in the sheet. We will also use Temboo to make the link between our project and Google Docs.

## Getting ready

There are some things you will need to do before you can take on this recipe. First, create a Google account if you haven't got one. Once this is done, create a new Google Docs spreadsheet. Name it `Galileo`, for example. Also, give a name to the first three columns corresponding to the data that we are going to log—`Date`, `Temperature`, and `Light Level`.

Then, go over to Temboo to create an account there too. We used Temboo in the previous chapter; it allows us to use web APIs with no difficulties. You can create an account by going to:

```
https://temboo.com/
```

If you need information about the Temboo library, go to:

```
https://www.temboo.com/library/Library/Google/Spreadsheets/
```

## How to do it...

We are now going to configure the different parts of the project so that we can log data in a Google Docs spreadsheet.

The first step is to create a new Google app, which we will use to log data in a spreadsheet. You can do this by going to:

```
https://console.developers.google.com
```

You can now create a new project:

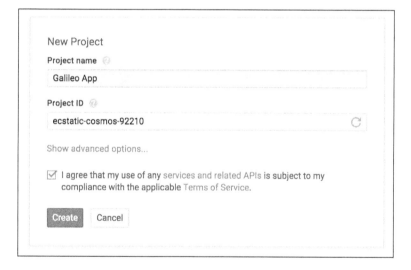

After that, you need to click on **APIs** and **Auth**, then on **APIs**, and activate the **Drive API**, as shown in this picture:

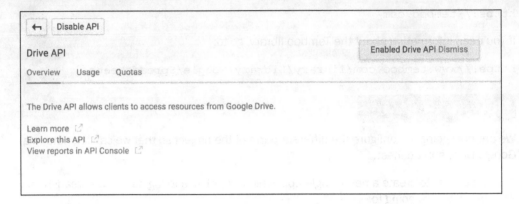

After that, click on **Credentials**. You will be taken to a page where you can find the **ClientID** that you will need later on Temboo.

Then, head over to Temboo at:

```
https://www.temboo.com/library/Library/Google/Spreadsheets/
```

You basically have to follow the instructions there to initialize the library. At some point, you will be asked to enter the **ClientID** you got before:

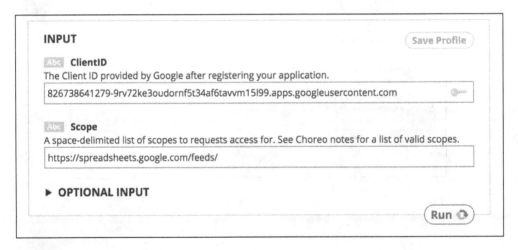

You will also be given a client secret key that you will also need in the rest of the recipe. Then, once the whole procedure is done, you will be given an **AccessToken**, which you need to enter here:

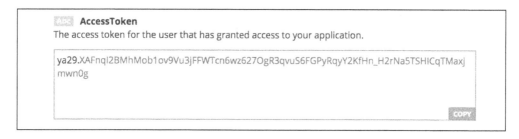

Note down this token; we will use it in a moment in our application.

We are now going to use Intel XDK again for the code for this recipe. This is the complete code:

```javascript
// Includes
var mraa = require("mraa");
var util = require('util');
var tsession = require("temboo/core/temboosession");
var session = new tsession.TembooSession("your_temboo_username",
"your_app_name", "your_app_key");

// Sensor pins
var temp_sensor_pin = new mraa.Aio(0);
temp_sensor_pin.setBit(12);
var light_sensor_pin = new mraa.Aio(1);
light_sensor_pin.setBit(12);

var Google = require("temboo/Library/Google/Spreadsheets");

var appendRowChoreo = new Google.AppendRow(session);

// Instantiate and populate the input set for the choreo
var appendRowInputs = appendRowChoreo.newInputSet();

function send_data() {

    // Measure light
    var a = light_sensor_pin.read();
    var light_level = a/4096*100;
    light_level = light_level.toPrecision(4);
    console.log("Light level: " + light_level + " %");

    // Measure temperature
    var b = temp_sensor_pin.read();
    var temperature = (b/4096*5000 - 500) / 10;
```

```
    temperature = temperature.toPrecision(4);
    console.log("Temperature: " + temperature + " C");

    // Date
    var d = new Date();
    var date = d.toString();

    // Set inputs (put your own Google app data here)
    appendRowInputs.set_ClientSecret("google_client_secret");
    appendRowInputs.set_RefreshToken("google_client_token");
    appendRowInputs.set_RowData(date + "," + temperature + "," +
light_level);
    appendRowInputs.set_SpreadsheetTitle("spreadsheet_title");
    appendRowInputs.set_ClientID("google_client_id");

    // Run the choreo, specifying success and error callback
handlers
    appendRowChoreo.execute(
        appendRowInputs,
        function(results){console.log(results.get_Response());},
        function(error){console.log(error.type);
console.log(error.message);}
    );
}

// Send data every 10 seconds
send_data();
setInterval(send_data, 10000);
```

There are several things you need to modify in this code. First, you need to enter your Temboo login, application name, and application key. This data can be found in your profile settings on Temboo.

Then, you need to enter data about your Google account—client ID, secret, and the access token you got before. Finally, you need to enter the name of the spreadsheet you created before.

You can now just copy this code and paste it into a new Intel XDK project. Refer to the previous chapter if you need more details on this procedure.

Don't forget to modify the `package.json` file, to specify that we are using the Temboo Node. js module.

Upload the code to the board, build it, and then execute it. After that, go to the spreadsheet you created before. You should see that the data is being logged in the spreadsheet:

| | A | B | C |
|---|---|---|---|
| 1 | Date | Temperature | Light Level |
| 2 | Tue Apr 21 2015 11:31:13 GMT+0000 (UTC) | 25.7 | 75.98 |
| 3 | Tue Apr 21 2015 11:31:24 GMT+0000 (UTC) | 25.7 | 76.27 |
| 4 | Tue Apr 21 2015 11:31:34 GMT+0000 (UTC) | 25.2 | 77.05 |
| 5 | Tue Apr 21 2015 11:31:44 GMT+0000 (UTC) | 25.2 | 77.73 |

Now, as you are in Google Sheets, you can also use the software's built-in functionalities to plot the data. To do that, simply select all the data (columns **A** to **C**), and click on **Insert Chart**. I chose a simple line plot for this project; here is the result:

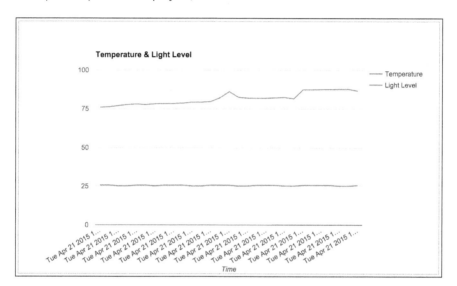

Note that, as this is in a Google Docs document, it is accessible from any web browser, so you can monitor this data from anywhere in the world!

## How it works...

This recipe uses Temboo to make the link between our Galileo board and the Google Drive API.

After we got the **AccessToken** from Temboo, we were able to log live measured data from the Galileo board in the Google Docs spreadsheet. Then, we simply used the built-in plotting functionalities of Google Sheets to plot the incoming data in real time.

## See also

I now recommend that you look at the next recipe to discover another way to monitor your Galileo board remotely, by using the MQTT protocol.

# Controlling your board from anywhere in the world

In this last recipe, we are going to see another way to control your Galileo projects from anywhere. Here, I use the word control, because we are actually going to use this recipe not only to monitor data remotely, but also to send commands to your board from the cloud. Of course, for this application, your board has to be connected to the Internet, via the Ethernet, for example.

We are going to use the MQTT protocol and a service called Lelylan to control our projects from anywhere in the world.

## Getting ready

The first step in this recipe is to create an account at Lelylan. This will allow us to control projects from anywhere in the world using a nice dashboard. To do this, go to:

```
http://lelylan.github.io/devices-dashboard-ng/#/
```

You will be redirected to your dashboard, where you can create a new device:

When asked about the device type, choose **Basic Light**. Choose **MQTT** for the protocol. Once the process is finished, you will be given a client or device **ID** and **SECRET** that you will need for the rest of this recipe:

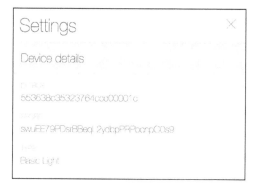

It's also time to connect a test device to your Galileo board for control purposes. I used a simple LED, but you can also use a relay, for example. Simply connect the device you want to test to pin number 7 on the Galileo board. If you want more information on how to connect a device to your Galileo board, refer to *Chapter 3, Controlling Hardware Devices*.

## How to do it...

We are now going to link the button in your dashboard to your Galileo board. This is the button in the dashboard:

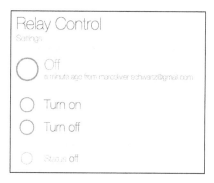

We are going to use the Intel XDK software to write the code for this recipe. This is the complete code:

```
// Device ID and secret
var device_id = "device_id";
var device_secret = "device_secret";
// Required modules
```

```
var m = require("mraa");
var util = require('util');
var mqtt   = require('mqtt');

var client = mqtt.createClient(1883, "178.62.108.47", {
    username: device_id,
    password: device_secret,
    clientId: "7393956449"
});

// Set output on pin 7
var myDigitalPin = new m.Gpio(7);
myDigitalPin.dir(m.DIR_OUT);

// Topics
in_topic  = 'devices/' + device_id + '/get';
out_topic = 'devices/' + device_id + '/set';

 // Connect event
client.on('connect', function () {
  client.subscribe(in_topic);
});

// When message is received
client.on('message', function (topic, message) {

  // Message is Buffer
  console.log(message.toString());

  json_data = JSON.parse(message.toString());

  // Check the status property value
  var value = json_data['properties'][0]['value']

  if (value == 'on') {
    myDigitalPin.write(1);
  }
  if (value == 'off') {
    myDigitalPin.write(0);
  }

  // Confirm to Lelylan
  client.publish(out_topic, message.toString())
});
```

Note that you need to change the device **SECRET** and the device **ID** in the code to the values you got from your dashboard.

You can now just copy this code and paste it into a new Intel XDK project. Refer to the previous chapter if you need more details on this procedure.

Don't forget to modify the `package.json` file, to specify that we are using the `mqtt` Node.js module.

Upload the code to the board, build it, and then execute it. After that, go to the dashboard again, and click on the button:

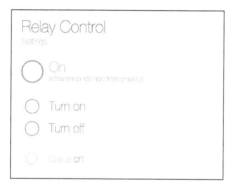

If you have an LED connected to pin number 7 for example, you should see that it turns on immediately. You will also see the confirmation in the dashboard (**Status on**).

## How it works...

This whole project is based on the MQTT protocol. MQTT is a lightweight protocol that was made specifically for the Internet of Things. You can learn more about it here:

`http://mqtt.org/`

The Lelylan dashboard provides a nice way to control devices that run the MQTT protocol, as is the case with the Galileo board.

## See also

You now have several tools that you can use to monitor data and control your Galileo board from anywhere in the world!

Note that you can also use the Intel Enable IoT project for similar functionalities.

# Troubleshooting cloud monitoring issues

The *Internet of Things* is a very interesting topic; however, there are always issues with the communication between your project and the cloud. This is why we are now going to look at the most common issues that can arise in the recipes found in this chapter.

## Dweet.io is not responding

The most common cause of not being able to get an answer from dweet.io is that the Internet connection on your Galileo board is not functioning properly. This can happen when the board is inactive for a long time. To solve this, simply reboot the board by clicking on the **REBOOT** button on the board itself, and then try to execute the project again.

## The dweet.io data does not appear in Freeboard.io

If no data appears on the dashboard, but you are sure that the data was logged correctly in dweet.io, there may be a problem with the datasource you defined. Make sure that you entered exactly the same `Thing` name in the Freeboard.io datasource. Then, make sure that you correctly linked this datasource to your dashboard widgets.

## Data is not being logged in my Google spreadsheet

If the Temboo project is running correctly but you cannot see anything being logged in the Google Docs spreadsheet, there are several things you can check.

First, check that you followed the Temboo procedure correctly to get your Google access token. Without the correct access token, the project won't work.

Then, make sure you authorized your Google application to access the Google Drive API.

Finally, make sure that you entered the name of your Google spreadsheet in the code. Also make sure that you gave a name to your columns inside this spreadsheet.

You can also test the choreo directly on the Temboo website, to check whether the problem is with your Galileo board or with Temboo.

## I cannot control my board from Lelylan

If you are running the code from the last recipe of this chapter, but nothing happens when you click the button, there are also several things you can check.

The first thing to check is that your Internet connection on the board is still active. Reboot the board if this is not the case.

Then, check if you get the confirmation message on the Lelylan dashboard. If so, you might simply have attached your test device (for example, the LED) to your board wrongly. If you think this is the case, check *Chapter 3, Controlling Hardware Devices* again.

Finally, also make sure that you correctly entered your Lelylan dashboard client **ID** and client **SECRET** in the JavaScript code running on your Galileo.

# 8

# Building a Home Automation System

In this chapter, we will cover the following recipes:

- ▶ Choosing the right components
- ▶ Building a Wi-Fi Arduino sensor module
- ▶ Connecting Arduino modules to the Galileo board
- ▶ Building an interface for your home automation system
- ▶ Connecting your home automation system to the Web
- ▶ Accessing your home automation system from anywhere
- ▶ Troubleshooting issues with your home automation system

## Introduction

In this last chapter, we are going to use everything that we have learned so far and apply it to building a home automation system based on the Galileo board. We are first going to see how to select the components for the project and how to build the system modules that will be based on Arduino.

Then, we are going to see how to connect these modules to the Galileo board, and how to build an interface for our system.

Finally, we will learn how to connect our home automation system to the Web and how to access it from anywhere.

# Choosing the right components

In this first recipe, we are going to see how to select the right components for your home automation system. Indeed, even if the Galileo board can do a lot by itself, it is not enough to build a complete home automation system. For example, you might want to have several sensors around your home in different rooms.

## Getting ready

The first step is to decide what you want from your home automation system. In this chapter, we are going to see how to connect the sensor modules, as an example. However, you may want other kinds of modules, such as modules to control appliances. Which modules? How many? These are the questions you'll need to answer before building your home automation system.

## How to do it...

As I mentioned before, the home automation system we are going to build in this chapter will be based on Arduino. We are going to use the most common Arduino board, the Arduino Uno, which is shown in this picture:

Then, you need a means of communication between the modules and the Galileo board, based on Arduino. There are many ways to do that, but here we are going to use a well-known communication medium—Wi-Fi.

To give Wi-Fi functionalities to Arduino, we are going to use a commonly used module—the CC3000 Wi-Fi chip. This is a picture of the module we are going to use:

We need a sensor to measure data. As an example, we are going to measure temperature and humidity on each module. To do this, we are going to use a DHT11 sensor, which is shown here:

Finally, we will also use jumper wires and breadboards to assemble the different modules.

## How it works...

We are going to have several modules based on Arduino as it is easy to program for the functionalities we want to achieve. They will all communicate via Wi-Fi with your router, and therefore with your Galileo board.

## See also

You can now move on to the next recipe to learn how to assemble and test your home automation modules.

# Building a Wi-Fi Arduino sensor module

In this recipe, we are going to learn how to build and test a Wi-Fi sensor module. Of course, if you want several of these, you can just repeat the steps.

## Getting ready

You will need to get all the components necessary to build an Arduino sensor module, as described in the first recipe. These are all the components required for this recipe:

- Arduino Uno board (`https://www.adafruit.com/product/50`)
- CC3000 Wi-Fi module (`https://www.adafruit.com/product/1510`)
- DHT11 (`https://www.adafruit.com/product/386`)
- Jumper wires (`https://www.adafruit.com/product/758`)
- Breadboard (`https://www.adafruit.com/products/64`)
- 10k ohm resistor

You will need the standard Arduino IDE for this project. You can get it from the following location:

`https://www.arduino.cc/en/Main/Software`

You will also need a few Arduino libraries for this recipe, and they are listed here as follows:

- aREST (`https://github.com/marcoschwartz/aREST`)
- Adafruit CC3000 library (`https://github.com/adafruit/Adafruit_CC3000_Library`)
- DHT library (`https://github.com/adafruit/DHT-sensor-library`)

To install a library, simply take the folder that you downloaded and save it in the Arduino libraries folder.

## How to do it...

We are now going to see how to assemble the sensor module.

Connect the IRQ pin on the CC3000 board to pin number 3 on the Arduino board, VBAT to pin 5, and CS to pin 10. Then, you need to connect the SPI pins to the Arduino board—MOSI, MISO, and CLK go to pins 11, 12, and 13, respectively. Finally, take care of the power supply— Vin goes to the Arduino 5V, and GND goes to GND.

The DHT sensor is easier to connect. Just plug in pin number 1 to the Arduino's 5V, pin number 4 to GND, and pin number 2 to Arduino pin 7. Finally, put the 10k resistor between sensor pins numbers 1 and 2.

The following picture illustrates the hardware connections:

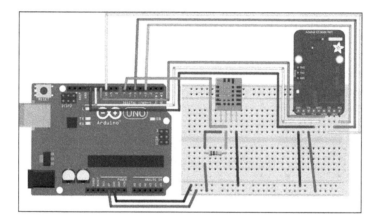

This is a picture of the assembled project:

It's now time to test our sensor module. You will need to copy this code and paste it into the Arduino IDE software. This is the complete code sketch for this project:

```
#define NUMBER_VARIABLES 2
#define NUMBER_FUNCTIONS 1

// Include required libraries
#include <Adafruit_CC3000.h>
#include <SPI.h>
#include <aREST.h>
#include "DHT.h"

// Define CC3000 chip pins
#define ADAFRUIT_CC3000_IRQ    3
#define ADAFRUIT_CC3000_VBAT   5
#define ADAFRUIT_CC3000_CS     10

// WiFi network (change with your settings !)
#define WLAN_SSID        "yourWiFiName"
#define WLAN_PASS        "yourWiFiPassword"
#define WLAN_SECURITY    WLAN_SEC_WPA2

// DHT11 sensor pins
#define DHTPIN 7
#define DHTTYPE DHT11

// Create CC3000 and DHT instances
DHT dht(DHTPIN, DHTTYPE);
Adafruit_CC3000 cc3000 = Adafruit_CC3000(ADAFRUIT_CC3000_CS,
ADAFRUIT_CC3000_IRQ, ADAFRUIT_CC3000_VBAT, SPI_CLOCK_DIV2);

// Create aREST instance
aREST rest = aREST();

// The port to listen for incoming TCP connections
#define LISTEN_PORT          80

// Server instance
Adafruit_CC3000_Server restServer(LISTEN_PORT);

// Variables to be exposed to the API
int temperature;
int humidity;
```

```
void setup(void)
{

  // Start Serial
  Serial.begin(115200);

  // Expose variables to REST API
  rest.variable("temperature",&temperature);
  rest.variable("humidity",&humidity);

  // Set name
  rest.set_id("1");
  rest.set_name("weather_station");

  // Initialize DHT sensor
  dht.begin();

  // Initialize the CC3000 module
  Serial.print("Initializing CC3000 ...");
  if (!cc3000.begin())
  {
    while(1);
  }
  Serial.println("done.");

  // Connect to  WiFi network
  Serial.print("Connecting to WiFi ...");
  cc3000.connectToAP(WLAN_SSID, WLAN_PASS, WLAN_SECURITY);
  Serial.println("done.");

  // Check DHCP
  Serial.print("Getting IP ...");
  while (!cc3000.checkDHCP())
  {
    delay(100);
  }
  Serial.println("done.");

  // Start server
  restServer.begin();

  displayConnectionDetails();
}
```

```
void loop(void)
{
  // Measure from DHT
  temperature = (uint8_t)dht.readTemperature();
  humidity = (uint8_t)dht.readHumidity();

  // Handle REST calls
  Adafruit_CC3000_ClientRef client = restServer.available();
  rest.handle(client);
}

bool displayConnectionDetails(void)
{
  uint32_t ipAddress, netmask, gateway, dhcpserv, dnsserv;

  if(!cc3000.getIPAddress(&ipAddress, &netmask, &gateway,
&dhcpserv, &dnsserv))
  {
    return false;
  }
  else
  {
    Serial.println(F("\nIP Addr: "));
cc3000.printIPdotsRev(ipAddress);
    return true;
  }
}
```

You need to modify a few things in this sketch. You need to enter your Wi-Fi name and password at the beginning of the sketch.

Then, you can just copy the code into the Arduino IDE, and upload it to the Arduino board. Don't forget to select **Arduino Uno** as the board type in the IDE, as you probably have the Galileo board selected.

Then, open the serial monitor. You will see some information about the board, and finally you will see the IP address that was assigned to the board, as shown in this screenshot:

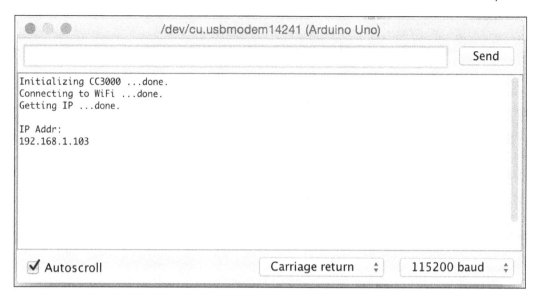

We can now test if we can access the temperature data. To do so, simply open your browser, and type:

```
http://192.168.1.103/temperature
```

You must replace the IP address with the address of your board. You should receive the following message:

```
{"temperature": 26, "id": "1", "name": "weather_station",
"connected": true}
```

If you can see this, congratulations, the sensor module is working!

## How it works...

The project is based on the aREST library, which is a library used for wireless communications on Arduino. It allows you to control the board completely using commands in any web browser, for example to get the temperature readings.

We are going to use the wireless communication libraries in the following recipes to read the data on the Arduino sensors modules from the Galileo board.

Note that, if you want to use several boards in your home automation system, you should give each board a different ID and name in the code.

You can now move on to the next recipe, in which we will see how to connect these Arduino modules to the Galileo board.

# Connecting Arduino modules to the Galileo board

In this recipe, we are going to establish a link between our Arduino Wi-Fi modules and the Galileo board. This is the first step in making the Galileo board the *hub* of our home automation system.

## Getting ready

The first step is to have at least one Arduino Wi-Fi module ready. You also need to have the Galileo board ready to run a Node.js program with the Intel XDK software, as in previous chapters.

## How to do it...

We are now going to examine the code to connect our Arduino boards to the Galileo board. We will assume here that we have two Arduino modules in our home automation system, at two different IP addresses: one ending with 103, and one ending with 105.

This is the complete code:

```
// Node-aREST
var rest = require("arest")(app);
rest.addDevice('http','192.168.1.103');
rest.addDevice('http','192.168.1.105');
```

Pretty simple, right? The only thing you need to change is the IP addresses of the boards in your system.

You also need to edit the `package.json` file to use the aREST Node.js module:

```
{
  "name": "Dashboard",
  "description": "",
  "version": "0.0.0",
  "main": "main.js",
  "engines": {
    "node": ">=0.10.0"
  },
```

```
    "dependencies": {
        "arest": "latest"
    }
}
```

You can now just copy this code and paste it into a new Intel XDK project. Refer to the previous chapter if you need more details on this procedure.

Don't forget to modify the `package.json` file. Upload the code to the board, build it, and then execute it. You should see that the two Arduino modules are added, with their respective IDs showing up in the console, as shown in this screenshot:

```
Listening on port 3000
Sending request to address: 192.168.1.103 for variable id
Sending request to address: 192.168.1.105 for variable id
Device added with ID: 2
Device added with ID: 1
```

We are now going to test the communication between the Galileo board and the Arduino modules. We want to read the temperature measured by the Arduino module number 1.

Assuming the IP address of your Galileo board is `192.168.1.101`, type this command in your browser:

```
http://192.168.1.101:3000/1/temperature
```

You should immediately receive the answer from the board:

`{"temperature":26,"id":"1","name":"weather_station","connected":true}`

If you can see this, it means that it works, and that there is now a link between your Galileo board and your Arduino modules.

## How it works...

In this recipe, we used the Node.js `Node-aREST` module, which can be interfaced with several Arduino modules.

The module queries every Arduino module declared in the code, and then adds it internally, so that they can be accessed from a single server, which is the Galileo board.

## See also

In the next recipe, we are going to build an interface based on this recipe, and monitor our Arduino sensors graphically.

# Building an interface for your home automation system

In the preceding recipe, we established a connection between our Arduino modules and the Galileo board, which is now acting as the hub for our home automation system.

However, what we would really like to do is have a nice graphical interface so that we can monitor our system, and this is exactly what we are going to do in this recipe.

## Getting ready

Before attempting this recipe, you need to complete the previous recipe, with at least one Arduino board connected to the Galileo board via Wi-Fi.

## How to do it...

This recipe is only about upgrading the code that we started to write in the preceding recipe. This is the complete code:

```
var express = require('express');
var app = express();

// Define port
var port = 3000;

// View engine
app.set('view engine', 'jade');

// Set public folder
app.use(express.static(__dirname + '/public'));

// Serve interface
app.get('/', function(req, res){
  res.render('interface');
});

// Node-aREST
var rest = require("arest")(app);
rest.addDevice('http','192.168.1.103');
rest.addDevice('http','192.168.1.105');

// Start server
app.listen(port);
console.log("Listening on port " + port);
```

This code makes use of the Express and Jade Node.js modules, which are very handy when creating graphical interfaces. Don't forget to add these dependencies into the `package.json` file.

We will then see how to code the interface itself. The interface is defined inside a Jade file, called `interface.jade`, and placed in a folder called `views`.

Jade is a templating language that allows us to write HTML with a much simpler code. This is the code that defines the interface for this recipe:

```
doctype
html
  head
    title Dashboard
    link(rel='stylesheet',
href="https://maxcdn.bootstrapcdn.com/bootstrap/3.3.0/css/bootstrap.min.css")
    link(rel='stylesheet', href="/css/demo.css")
    script(src="https://code.jquery.com/jquery-2.1.1.min.js")
    script(src="/js/demo.js")
    script(src="
http://cdn.rawgit.com/Foliotek/AjaxQ/master/ajaxq.js")
  body
    .container
      h1 Home Automation Interface
      .row.voffset30.text30
        .col-md-3
          div Sensor 1
        .col-md-4
          div Temperature:
            span#temperature1
        .col-md-4
          div Humidity:
            span#humidity1
        .col-md-1
          div#status1
      .row.voffset30.text30
        .col-md-3
          div Sensor 2
        .col-md-4
          div Temperature:
            span#temperature2
        .col-md-4
          div Humidity:
            span#humidity2
        .col-md-1
          div#status2
```

We are basically defining two indicators (temperature and humidity) per Arduino module.

Finally, we need to link the interface to the Node.js server. This is done with a piece of JavaScript code, defined in a file called `demo.js`, and stored inside the folder `public/js`. This is the complete code:

```javascript
$(document).ready(function() {

    // Timeout
    $.ajaxSetup({
        timeout: 1500 //Time in milliseconds
    });

    // Refresh data in the interface
    function refreshData(device_id, variable) {
        $.getq('queue', '/' + device_id +'/' + variable,
function(json_data) {

            // Temperature
            if (json_data[variable]){
            $("#" + variable + device_id).text(json_data[variable]);
            }

            // Status
            if (json_data.connected){
              $("#status" + device_id).text('Online');
              $("#status" + device_id).css('color', 'green');
            }
            else {
              $("#status" + device_id).text('Offline');
              $("#status" + device_id).css('color', 'red');
            }

        }).fail(function(){
            $("#status" + device_id).text('Offline');
          $("#status" + device_id).css('color', 'red');
        });
    }

    // Refresh interface at the start
    refreshData("1", "temperature");
    refreshData("2", "temperature");
    refreshData("1", "humidity");
    refreshData("2", "humidity");
```

```
  // Refresh every 10 seconds
  setInterval(function() {refreshData("1", "temperature");},
10000);
  setInterval(function() {refreshData("2", "temperature");},
10000);
  setInterval(function() {refreshData("1", "humidity");}, 10000);
  setInterval(function() {refreshData("2", "humidity");}, 10000);

  });
```

This will refresh the indicators inside the interface every 10 seconds.

You can now just copy this code and paste it into a new Intel XDK project. However, I recommend you get it from the GitHub repository, at the following location:

```
https://github.com/marcoschwartz/galileo-cookbook
```

Upload the code to the board, build it, and then execute it. You can now go to the IP address of the board, at:

```
http://galileo_ip_address:3000
```

You should immediately see the interface with the data of both modules displayed:

| Home Automation Interface | | | |
| --- | --- | --- | --- |
| Sensor 1 | Temperature: 27 | Humidity: 31 | Online |
| Sensor 2 | Temperature: 22 | Humidity: 39 | Online |

If you can see that, it means that your Galileo board is grabbing live data from your Arduino Wi-Fi modules, and displaying it in the interface.

## How it works...

In this project, we built on top of what we did in the previous recipe to add a graphical interface to our project.

We used two Node.js modules to do that. The first one was Express, as used previously, and that allowed us to give some structure to our web server.

Then, we used Jade to write our graphical interface. We also added some JavaScript to make the link between the interface and the Node.js server.

## See also

You can now go to the next two recipes, which will allow you to go even further with your home automation system by connecting it to the Web.

# Connecting your home automation system to the Web

In this recipe, we are going to connect our home automation system to the Web. It's great to have Wi-Fi modules measuring temperature and humidity, but it would be cool to have the outside temperature displayed as well.

We are going to simply upgrade the interface that we created in the previous chapter as we don't want to have another Wi-Fi module outside of your home, so that it grabs the data from the Web and displays it in the same interface.

## Getting ready

In order to complete this recipe, you will need to have finished the previous recipe and have the home automation system running with the graphical interface.

## How to do it...

We are now going to see how to modify the different files from the previous recipe so that we can display the external temperature and humidity at your location.

First, the interface. We simply add another row to the interface, with two indicators; one indicator for the external temperature, and the other for the humidity. This is what you need to add into the interface:

```
.row.voffset30.text30
  .col-md-3
    div External
  .col-md-4
    div Temperature:
      span#ext_temp
  .col-md-4
    div Humidity:
      span#ext_humidity
```

Then, we need to modify the JavaScript file to grab data from OpenWeatherMap, which is a service we will use to grab the weather data at your location. This is what you need to add in the JavaScript code:

```
$.ajax({
    url:
"http://api.openweathermap.org/data/2.5/weather?q=lublin,poland",
    crossDomain: true
}).done(function(result) {
    $("#ext_temp").html((result.main.temp -  273.15).toFixed(2));
    $("#ext_humidity").html(result.main.humidity);
});
```

Of course, you will need to modify the code with your own location.

Next, run the code on your Galileo board, and go back to the interface. This is what you should see:

| Home Automation Interface | | | |
|---|---|---|---|
| Sensor 1 | Temperature: 26 | Humidity: 32 | Online |
| Sensor 2 | Temperature: 22 | Humidity: 39 | Online |
| External | Temperature: 11.95 | Humidity: 75 | |

As you can see, we now have the weather data displayed in the same interface as the measurements from the Arduino Wi-Fi boards.

## How it works...

This recipe is based on the service provided by OpenWeatherMap, which offers a free API to get precise weather data at the location of your choice. It is very easy to integrate with our project based on Node.js, so we use the data from this website to display the outside temperature and humidity without having to put a sensor outside.

## See also

You can now go to the next recipe to learn how to access your home automation system from anywhere in the world.

# Accessing your home automation system from anywhere

In this last recipe, we are going to see how to access your home automation system from anywhere in the world. To do this, we are going to use the Ngrok software that will allow us to *tunnel* a connection to your home automation system from the outside.

## Getting ready

For this recipe, you will need the project from the previous recipe running on your Galileo board.

The first step is to get the Ngrok software. You can get it from the following location:

```
https://ngrok.com/
```

Carefully follow the installation instructions for your operating system. The goal at the end is to have Ngrok installed on your computer and to be able to access it from a terminal.

Note that all the data will go through the Ngrok servers, so if you have sensitive data on your Galileo board or your board is used to control important devices, this might be something to think about.

Of course, your board also needs to be connected to the Internet at this point.

## How to do it...

Use a terminal to navigate to the folder where Ngrok is installed. Then, type the following:

```
./ngrok 192.168.1.103:3000
```

You need to change the IP address to the IP address of your Galileo board, as used previously.

Then, you should see the following in your terminal:

```
ngrok                                                      (Ctrl+C to quit)

Tunnel Status              online
Version                    1.7/1.7
Forwarding                 http://4681858b.ngrok.com -> 192.168.1.103:3000
Forwarding                 https://4681858b.ngrok.com -> 192.168.1.103:3000
Web Interface              127.0.0.1:4040
# Conn                     0
Avg Conn Time              0.00ms
```

See this **Forwarding** URL? This is the one you will need to access your home automation system from anywhere in the world. Just go there using any web browser, and you should see your home automation system interface:

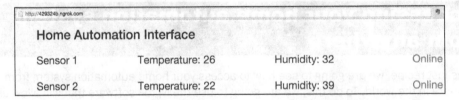

Note that this can be accessed from anywhere, so you can monitor your home wherever you are.

## How it works...

This recipe is entirely based on the Ngrok software, which can be used to make any web server accessible outside of your local Wi-Fi network.

Here, we use it to make the web server running on your Galileo accessible from the outside world, and therefore make your home automation system accessible from anywhere.

## See also

You have completed this chapter now, so you can experiment and add more modules to your home automation system. For example, you can add motion sensor modules or other modules to control electrical appliances. You can also use this project to control the air conditioning in your home, according to the measured temperature.

# Troubleshooting issues with your home automation system

As you build your own home automation system with the Galileo board, you may encounter technical issues. This section is designed to assist you with some of the most common problems.

## My Arduino Wi-Fi module can't connect to the Wi-Fi network

If you have built your Arduino module but cannot make it connect to your Wi-Fi network, there are several things you can check. First, make sure that you entered your Wi-Fi network name and password correctly.

Then, carefully follow the hardware connection instructions at the beginning of this chapter. Finally, make sure that you have the latest versions of all the libraries mentioned earlier.

## The Galileo board can't communicate with the Arduino modules

If you are at the stage when you want to connect your Arduino Wi-Fi modules to your Galileo board, but you get an error message in the console, there are several things you can check.

First, make sure that you entered the correct IP address in the JavaScript code, so that the Galileo board is accessing the right Arduino modules. Then, make sure that every module is working individually by running the test commands that you can find in the corresponding recipes.

## The graphical interface is not displayed

If you managed to link the Arduino Wi-Fi modules to your Intel Galileo board but the interface is not displayed correctly, or not at all, there are several things that could be wrong.

First, make sure that you modified the `package.json` file correctly so that it includes the Express and Jade Node.js modules.

Then, make sure you are accessing your server with the correct IP address.

Finally, use the code from the GitHub repository to ensure you have the correct files in the correct folders.

## The external weather data is not displayed

If the external weather data is not displayed in the interface, and you have followed all the instructions, it may be that the Internet connection on the Galileo board is down.

To solve this problem, simply reboot the board by clicking on the right button on the board.

# Index

## A

**Adafruit**
references, for Arduino sensor module
requisites 132
**Adafruit CC3000 library**
URL 132
**Advanced Linux Sound Architecture
(ALSA) drivers 6**
**analog sensor**
connecting 23-25
**API**
accessing, via Temboo 85-88
creating, for Galileo 67-71
**application issues**
troubleshooting 89
**Arduino IDE**
using, with Galileo board 20-22
**Arduino modules**
connecting, to Galileo board 138, 139
**Arduino Motor Shield**
URL 40
**Arduino XBee shield**
URL 43
**aREST**
URL 132

## B

**board**
controlling 122-125

## C

**cloud device**
data, sending to 110-113

## cloud monitoring
hardware, building for 107-110
hardware, testing for 107-110
issues, troubleshooting 126, 127
**common issues**
with hardware devices,
troubleshooting 53, 54
with sensors, troubleshooting 35

## D

**dashboard**
data, monitoring remotely 113-116
**data**
logging, in local database 94-98
logging, in online datasheet 116-121
sending, to cloud device 110-113
**DC motor**
connecting 40-42
**DHT library**
URL 132
**digital sensor**
connecting 26-28
**dweet.io**
about 111
URL 111

## E

**Enable IoT**
URL 113
**Express**
about 60
URL 60
using, on Galileo 60, 61

## F

**Facebook**
  URL 82
**file-sharing server**
  creating 74, 75
**Forecast.io**
  URL 75
**Freeboard.io**
  about 116
  URL 113

## G

**Galileo**
  accessing, via Wi-Fi 13-15
  configuring 2-4
**Galileo board**
  accessing remotely 9, 10
  Arduino IDE, using with 20-22
  Arduino modules, connecting to 138, 139
  tweeting from 77-80

## H

**hardware**
  building, for cloud monitoring 107-110
  testing, for cloud monitoring 107-110
**highcharts library**
  URL 98
**home automation system**
  accessing, from anywhere 145, 146
  connecting, to Web 144, 145
  interface, building for 140-143
  right components, selecting 130-132
  troubleshooting issues 147, 148

## I

**I2C LCD screen**
  URL 29
**Intel Galileo**
  about 22
  URL 22
**Intel XDK software**
  download link 56

using 56, 57
working 58
**Inter-Integrated Circuits (I2C) protocol 28**
**Internet of Things (IoT) 107**
**IoT Linux image**
  about 9
  download link 7
  using 6-8
  working 8

## J

**jumper wires**
  URL 23

## L

**LCD screen**
  connecting 28-31
  temperature, displaying on 31-34
**Lelylan**
  URL 122
**Linux installation issues**
  troubleshooting 16, 17
**live data visualization 102-105**
**local database**
  data, logging in 94-98

## M

**measured data**
  accessing, remotely 92-94
**measurements**
  displaying, stored in database 98-101
**modules**
  installing 11, 12
  updating 12
**MongoDB**
  URL 95
**Mongoose Node.js module**
  URL 97
**MQTT protocol**
  URL 125
**mraa module**
  URL 64

## N

**Ngrok**
URL 146
**Node.js**
URL 93

## O

**online datasheet**
data, logging in 116-121

## P

**pins**
controlling, via web server 64-67
reading, via web server 62-64
**Polulu 5V relay module**
URL 38
**PuTTY**
about 10
URL 10

## R

**relay**
connecting 38, 39

## S

**SD card reader**
using, to log data 49-52
**Secure Shell (SSH) 9**
**sensors issues**
troubleshooting 105
**servomotor**
controlling, from rotating knob 46-48
**simple Linux image**
about 6
download link 5
features 6
using 4, 5
**simple Node.js server**
running 58, 59
**simple PIR motion sensor**
URL 26

## Sparkfun
references, for cloud monitoring
requisites 108

## T

**Temboo**
APIs, accessing via 85-88
URL 117
web APIs, accessing via 80-85
**temperature**
displaying, on LCD screen 31-34
**TMP36 sensor**
URL 23
**troubleshooting**
issues with hardware devices 53, 54
issues with sensors 35
Linux installation issues 16, 17
web server issues 71, 72
**Twilio 88**
**twit module**
URL 79
**Twitter**
URL 78

## U

**USB XBee explorer module**
URL 43

## W

**weather data**
accessing, remotely 75-77
**Web**
home automation system,
connecting to 144, 145
**web APIs**
accessing, via Temboo 80-85
**web server**
creating 55
issues, troubleshooting 71, 72
**Wi-Fi Arduino sensor module**
building 132-137

# X

## Thank you for buying
## Intel Galileo Networking Cookbook

# About Packt Publishing

Packt, pronounced 'packed', published its first book, *Mastering phpMyAdmin for Effective MySQL Management*, in April 2004, and subsequently continued to specialize in publishing highly focused books on specific technologies and solutions.

Our books and publications share the experiences of your fellow IT professionals in adapting and customizing today's systems, applications, and frameworks. Our solution-based books give you the knowledge and power to customize the software and technologies you're using to get the job done. Packt books are more specific and less general than the IT books you have seen in the past. Our unique business model allows us to bring you more focused information, giving you more of what you need to know, and less of what you don't.

Packt is a modern yet unique publishing company that focuses on producing quality, cutting-edge books for communities of developers, administrators, and newbies alike. For more information, please visit our website at www.packtpub.com.

# About Packt Open Source

In 2010, Packt launched two new brands, Packt Open Source and Packt Enterprise, in order to continue its focus on specialization. This book is part of the Packt open source brand, home to books published on software built around open source licenses, and offering information to anybody from advanced developers to budding web designers. The Open Source brand also runs Packt's open source Royalty Scheme, by which Packt gives a royalty to each open source project about whose software a book is sold.

# Writing for Packt

We welcome all inquiries from people who are interested in authoring. Book proposals should be sent to author@packtpub.com. If your book idea is still at an early stage and you would like to discuss it first before writing a formal book proposal, then please contact us; one of our commissioning editors will get in touch with you.

We're not just looking for published authors; if you have strong technical skills but no writing experience, our experienced editors can help you develop a writing career, or simply get some additional reward for your expertise.

## Internet of Things with Intel Galileo

ISBN: 978-1-78217-458-5          Paperback: 212 pages

Employ the Intel Galileo board to design a world of smarter technology for your home

1. Discover some of Galileo's best development options using Arduino and Node.js.

2. Build complex projects in the field of Internet of Things and integrate with IoT platforms.

3. A step-by-step guide that takes you from the basics of IoT to developing full fledged systems that can be put into daily use.

## Arduino Development Cookbook

ISBN: 978-1-78398-294-3          Paperback: 246 pages

Over 50 hands-on recipes to quickly build and understand Arduino projects, from the simplest to the most extraordinary

1. Get quick, clear guidance on all the principle aspects of integration with the Arduino.

2. Learn the tools and components needed to build engaging electronics with the Arduino.

3. Make the most of your board through practical tips and tricks.

Please check **www.PacktPub.com** for information on our titles

# Home Automation with Intel Galileo

ISBN: 978-1-78528-577-6        Paperback: 188 pages

Create thrilling and intricate home automation projects using Intel Galileo

1. Make the most out of Intel Galileo by understanding its fundamentals and architecture.

2. Explore sensors and devices to successfully control home functions like lights, security, energy management, and many more.

3. Written in a lucid and step-by-step approach explaining varied aspects of home automation.

# Intel Galileo Essentials

ISBN: 978-1-78439-890-3        Paperback: 162 pages

Leverage the power of Intel Galileo to construct amazingly simple, yet impressive projects

1. Learn how to connect additional hardware to the Intel Galileo to easily create complex robots.

2. Understand GPIO pins on the Galileo and how to use them.

3. Control a DC motor so that your unit can drive wheels or tracks.

Please check **www.PacktPub.com** for information on our titles